Aussicht vom »Treptower« die Spree entlang über die Oberbaumbrücke hinweg in Richtung Berlin-Mitte.
A view along the river Spree from the top of the Treptowers Office Centre towards the Mitte district over the Oberbaumbrücke.

Blick vom Palace Hotel auf die City West mit der Kaiser-Wilhelm-Gedächtniskirche – links davon der Kurfürstendamm, rechts die Budapester Straße.
*View of the western part of the city from the Palace Hotel, with the Kaiser-
Wilhelm-Gedächtniskirche (Memorial Church). The street known as Kurfürstendamm extends to the left; the Budapester Strasse is at right.*

BERLIN

IM BILD

ERIK-JAN OUWERKERK (FOTOGRAFIE)
MIT TEXTEN VON ANDREAS KRAUSE
UND ANTONIA MEINERS

deutsch | english

BERLIN

nicolai

CONTENTS

INHALT

FOREWORD by Antonia Meiners

There's only one Berlin / And yet while the world still spins / And while each new day begins / There's only one Berlin

So sang Claire Waldoff, one of Berlin's most popular cabaret artistes, in the "golden Twenties". Despite soaring inflation, despite radicalized political conflict, Berlin was a cosmopolitan city like no other at that time. The imperial residence, whose population has risen from 900,000 in 1871 to what was now four million, became the capital of the republic: a cultural and financial centre, and a magnet for both the artistic and the scientific avant-garde. The cityscape changed, tenements sprang up; beside them were generously disposed housing estates by architects like Max Taut, and beside the Wilhelminian show buildings were modern functional structures in glass and steel by Walter Gropius, Erich Mendelsohn and others.

Before 1933, no one had an inkling of the suffering the German capital would have to face in the 20th century. Numerous buildings from the imperial period had already been pulled down from the mid thirties onwards for the "World Capital City Germania" planned by Hitler's architect Albert Speer. At the end of the Second World War, after five years of bombing terror, Berlin did not seem capable of surviving. Almost half of the over 1.5 million dwellings had been destroyed, and Berlin's central districts were just one big expanse of rubble.

Rebuilding took place in a divided city, one Berlin became two, separated by a concrete wall 40 kilometres long, and the centre remained a wilderness with the border between East and West running through it. Waldoff's song seemed to make sense only in terms of a nostalgic look back.

Then came a colossal change, suddenly and in a way no one had foreseen. The Wall fell on 9 November 1989, Germany was reunited and Berlin became its capital again. In the nineties it was transformed into a gigantic building site, major architectural projects like Potsdamer Platz and spectacular buildings like the Jewish Museum were realized; extensive restoration began in the old residential quarters dating back to the imperial period. Many projects have now been concluded that a number of people thought would drag on for decades. Berlin is resplendent in new glory: a modern capital, an open-minded 21st century metropolis — and one Berlin again.

Erik-Jan Ouwerkerk's photographs show the new face of the city, this incomparable mixture of historical architectural monuments, modern architecture and effervescent cultural life. His images are complemented by detailed essays and historical photographs, making the past visible for the reader in the present. And finally at the end of the book Andreas Krause writes about the history of the city and his view of Ouwerkerk's pictures.

VORWORT von Antonia Meiners

Es gibt nur ein Berlin / Und so lang die Welt sich dreht / Und so lang die Zeit vergeht / Gibt es nur ein Berlin

So sang es einst Claire Waldoff, in den »goldenen zwanziger Jahren« eine der populärsten Chansonette auf den Berliner Kabarettbühnen. Trotz dramatisch steigender Inflation, trotz Radikalisierung der politischen Auseinandersetzungen war Berlin damals Weltstadt wie kaum eine andere. Aus der kaiserlichen Residenz, deren Einwohnerzahl nach 1871 von 900 000 auf inzwischen vier Millionen angewachsen war, wurde die Hauptstadt der Republik: ein kulturelles und wirtschaftliches Zentrum und ein Sammelbecken sowohl künstlerischer als auch wissenschaftlicher Avantgarde. Das Stadtbild veränderte sich, neben Mietskasernen entstanden großzügig angelegte Siedlungen von Architekten wie Max Taut, neben wilhelminischen Prunkbauten modern-sachliche Gebäude aus Glas und Stahl von Walter Gropius, Erich Mendelsohn und anderen.

Wohl kaum jemand ahnte vor 1933, welches Leid der deutschen Hauptstadt im Verlauf des 20. Jahrhunderts noch bevorstand. Schon Mitte der dreißiger Jahre wurden für die von Hitlers Architekt Albert Speer geplante »Welthauptstadt Germania« zahlreiche Bauten aus der Kaiserzeit abgerissen. Am Ende des Zweiten Weltkriegs, nach fünf Jahren Bombenterror, schien Berlin nicht mehr lebensfähig. Von 1,5 Millionen Wohnungen waren mehr als die Hälfte zerstört, Berlins Innenstadt-

bezirke ein einziges Trümmerfeld. Der Wiederaufbau erfolgte getrennt, aus einer Stadt wurden zwei, geschieden durch eine 40 Kilometer lange Betonmauer, und die Mitte, durchzogen von der Grenze zwischen Ost- und Westberlin, blieb Ödnis. Waldoffs Lied schien nur noch für einen nostalgischen Rückblick tauglich.

Dann kam die plötzliche und so von niemanden vorhergesehene Wende. Am 9. November 1989 fiel die Mauer, Deutschland wurde eins und Berlin wieder Hauptstadt. In den neunziger Jahren mutierte sie zu einer riesigen Baustelle, es entstanden architektonische Großprojekte wie der Potsdamer Platz und spektakuläre Gebäude wie das Jüdische Museum, und in den alten Wohnquartieren aus der Kaiserzeit begannen umfangreiche Restaurierungen. Inzwischen sind viele der Vorhaben abgeschlossen, von denen so mancher dachte, dass sie sich über Jahrzehnte hinziehen würden. Berlin erstrahlt in neuem Glanz, ist moderne Hauptstadt und weltoffene Metropole des 21. Jahrhunderts – und auch wieder *ein Berlin*.

Die Fotografien Erik-Jan Ouwerkerks zeigen das neue Gesicht der Stadt, diese unvergleichliche Mischung aus historischen Baudenkmälern, moderner Architektur und lebendigem kulturellem Leben. Ergänzt werden sie mit ausführlichen Texten und historischen Aufnahmen, die für den Leser das Vergangene im Heutigen sichtbar machen. Am Ende des Buches schließlich erzählt Andreas Krause von der Historie der Stadt und von seiner Sicht auf die Bilder Ouwerkerks.

Das Brandenburger Tor – bekanntestes Wahrzeichen Berlins. Seit über zweihundert Jahren bildet es am Pariser Platz den Abschluss des Boulevards Unter den Linden zum Tiergarten hin.
The Brandenburg Gate – Berlin's most famous landmark. It has marked the Tiergarten end of the boulevard Unter den Linden in Pariser Platz for over two hundred years.

Das Brandenburger Tor wurde 1791 nach Entwürfen des Architekten Carl Gotthard Langhans fertig gestellt. Von Beginn an war das prächtige klassizistische Stadttor ein Wahrzeichen für die wechselvolle Geschichte der Hauptstadt. Schon 1806 ritt hier Kaiser Napoleon im Triumphzug nach Berlin ein und ließ die Quadriga als Beutegut nach Paris transportieren – von wo sie die Preußen 1815 wieder nach Hause holten. Fortan galt die Schadow'sche Friedensgöttin als Siegesgöttin. In den folgenden Epochen glänzten unter ihrem Streitwagen preußische und kaiserliche Uniformen bei ihren Siegesparaden. Als 1933 Hitlers SA hier aufmarschierte und das »Tausendjährige Reich« verkündete, begann das dunkelste Kapitel Deutschlands, das schon zwölf Jahre später in einer Katastrophe endete. Im Mai 1945 hissten die Sieger über Hitler-

deutschland ihre Fahne auf der Quadriga. Berlin wurde eine Vier-Mächte-Stadt, und bald trennte das Brandenburger Tor Ost und West, wurde zum Symbol des Kalten Krieges. Erst nach dem Mauerfall 1989 rückte es wieder in die Mitte des vereinten Berlins und ist inzwischen einer der beliebtesten Anziehungspunkte für Besucher aus aller Welt.

The Brandenburg Gate was designed by the architect Carl Gotthard Langhans and completed in 1791. The magnificent neo-classical city gate symbolized the city's chequered history from the outset. The Emperor Napoleon rode into Berlin in triumph here as early as 1806, and had the Quadriga conveyed to Paris as booty – the Prussians retrieved it in 1815. Schadow's peace goddess was seen as a goddess

Das Brandenburger Tor, gekrönt von der Quadriga. Die Plastik entstand nach einem Entwurf des Berliner Bildhauers Johann Gottfried Schadow.
The Brandenburg Gate, topped by the Quadriga. The sculpture was designed by the Berlin sculptor Johann Gottfried Schadow.

Soldaten der Volksarmee sperren den Durchgang am Brandenburger Tor am 14. August 1961, einen Tag, nachdem die DDR ihre Grenzen geschlossen hat.
Soldiers from the Volksarmee block the way through the Brandenburg Gate on 14 August 1961, one day after the GDR closed the borders.

of victory from then on. Prussian and Imperial uniforms glittered under her chariot in the victory parades of subsequent epochs. Germany's darkest chapter started here when Hitler's SA marched past and proclaimed the "Thousand-Year Reich", ending in catastrophe only twelve years later. The victors over Hitler's Germany hoisted their flag on the Quadriga in May 1945. Berlin became a four-power city, and soon the Brandenburg Gate was dividing East and West, and came to symbolize the Cold War. It did not shift back into the centre of a united Berlin until the Wall fell in 1989, and is now one of the most popular attractions for visitors from all over the world.

Panorama-Installation der »Gruppe 180« auf dem Pariser Platz im Mai/Juni 2005, 60 Jahre nach dem Ende des Zweiten Weltkriegs.
Panorama installation by "Group 180" in Pariser Platz in May/June 2005, 60 years after the end of the Second World War.

Der Pariser Platz, heute ein Spiegel zeitgenössischer Architektur, wurde im 19. Jahrhundert gern als »Salon von Berlin« bezeichnet. Gründe dafür waren zum einen seine bevorzugte Lage gleich hinter dem Brandenburger Tor und zum anderen die vornehmen und berühmten Bewohner der noblen Adelspaläste und Bürgerhäuser, die einst sein Karree säumten. Unter anderem hatte hier der Maler Max Liebermann sein Atelier, der den Besuchern gern den Weg erklärte: »Wenn de reinkommst nach Berlin, gleich links.« Entstanden war der Pariser Platz um 1734 als »Quarrée« – gemeinsam mit dem »Octogon« (Leipziger Platz) und dem

»Rondell« (später Belle-Alliance-Platz, heute Mehringplatz); ihre Umbenennung erfolgte 1814 in Erinnerung an den Sieg über Napoleon. Am Ende des Zweiten Weltkriegs standen nur noch wenig Gebäude auf dem Pariser Platz, letzte Überreste fielen nach dem Mauerbau 1961, da das Gebiet zu den Grenzanlagen gehörte. Nach der deutschen Einheit wurde in den neunziger Jahren mit der Neubebauung des Platzes begonnen, die nach Fertigstellung der Amerikanischen Botschaft an der Südwestecke abgeschlossen sein wird.

Im Mai 2005 wurde am Pariser Platz 4 der Neubau des Gebäudes der Akademie der Künste von Günter Behnisch eröffnet.
Günter Behnisch's new building for the Academy of Arts opened in May 2005 at 4 Pariser Platz.

Pariser Platz, now a mirror for contemporary architecture, was affectionately known as "Berlin's drawing room" in the 19th century. This was because of its privileged location immediately beyond the Brandenburg Gate, and also the distinguished and famous occupants of the noble palaces and town houses that once stood around it. These included the painter Max Liebermann, who had his studio here, and enjoyed telling visitors how to get there: "When you get into Berlin, just on the left." Pariser Platz was built as a "Quarrée" around 1734 – at the same time as the "Octogon" (Leipziger Platz) and the "Rondell" (later Belle-

Alliance-Platz); it was rechristened in 1814 to commemorate the victory over Napoleon.
Few buildings were standing in Pariser Platz at the end of the Second World War. The remainder fell after the Wall was built in 1961, as the area was part of the border constructions. Work on rebuilding the square started in the 1990s after German reunification; it will be completed when the American Embassy is finished in the south-west corner.

Das »Adlon« an der Südostecke des Pariser Platzes. Bei der Gestaltung des 1997 eröffneten Luxushotels orientierten sich die Architekten Patzschke, Klotz & Partner an dem legendären Vorgängerbau von 1907.
The "Adlon" on the south-east corner of Pariser Platz. The architects Patzschke, Klotz & Partner took its legendary 1907 predecessor as their model when the luxury hotel reopened in 1997.

Konferenzraum im Atrium des von Frank O. Gehry entworfenen Bankgebäudes am Pariser Platz 3.
Conference room in the atrium of the bank designed by Frank O. Gehry at 3 Pariser Platz.

Südlich vom Brandenburger Tor erhebt sich das Stelenfeld des Denkmals für die ermordeten Juden Europas mit dem darunter liegenden Ort der Information. Nach Entwürfen des amerikanischen Architekten Peter Eisenman war mit den Arbeiten im Frühjahr 2003 begonnen worden; am 10. Mai 2005 konnte es der Öffentlichkeit übergeben werden. Das aus 2711 unterschiedlich hohen Betonstelen errichtete Mahnmal bedeckt ein Gebiet, das einst zu den wichtigsten Ministerien des Kaiserreichs und später der Nationalsozialisten gehörte. Das Areal zwischen der Bebauung am Pariser Platz und der Voßstraße, an der Hitlers Reichskanzlei stand, war geprägt von den Ministergärten.

Sie gehörten zu den Ministerien und Regierungsgebäuden, die die Wilhelmstraße säumten. Nördlich des Denkmals, an der Behrenstraße, befand sich die Dienstvilla von Joseph Goebbels. Die Gärten und die im Krieg zerstörten Gebäude, die nun im Grenzgebiet lagen, wurden nach dem Mauerbau im Jahr 1961 eingeebnet.

The field of stelae for the Memorial to the Murdered Jews in Europe with the Information Centre under it is south of the Brandenburg Gate. Work started on the memorial designed by the American architect Peter Eisenman in spring 2003, and it was opened to the public on 10 May

Blick auf die DDR-Grenzanlagen, September 1984; etwa dort, wo der Grenzturm gleich neben den Bäumen sichtbar ist, befindet sich heute das Stelenfeld des Denkmals.
View of the GDR border, in September 1984; the memorial's field of stelae are now roughly where the border watchtower is visible just by the trees.

2005. The monument consists of 2711 concrete stelae of different heights, and covers an area that used to belong to the major ministries in the imperial period, and later under the National Socialists. The site between the development in Pariser Platz and Vossstrasse, where Hitler's Reich Chancellery stood, was noted for the Ministergärten (ministers' gardens). They belonged to the ministries and government buildings in Wilhelmstrasse. North of the monument, in Behrenstrasse, was Joseph Goebbels's official villa. The gardens and the buildings damaged in war were razed to the ground after the Wall was built in 1961, as they were now in the border area.

Das Denkmal für die ermordeten Juden Europas an der Ebertstraße;
Teil des Stelenfeldes.
*Memorial to the Murdered Jews in Europe in Ebertstrasse;
part of the field of stelae.*

Mit dem Bau der Französischen Friedrichstadtkirche für die Berliner Hugenotten und der gegenüberliegenden lutherischen deutschen Kirche begann um 1700 die Geschichte des Gendarmenmarkts; seinen Namen hatte er unter dem Soldatenkönig aufgrund der hiesigen Stallungen für das Regiment »Gens d'Armes« bekommen. Friedrich der Große ließ die Kirchen 1780–85 von Architekt Karl von Gontard mit den prachtvollen, aufeinander bezogenen Turmbauten errichten, von nun an Deutscher und Französischer Dom genannt. Zwischen ihnen entstand ein »Französisches Comödienhaus«, das sich unter Friedrich Wilhelm II. zum »Königlichen Nationaltheater« wandelte und 1802 einen Neubau erhielt. Hier spielte man Lessing, Goethe, Schiller, Mozarts »Zauberflöte« und E.T.A. Hoffmanns Oper »Undine«. E.T.A. Hoffmanns bevorzugtes Weinlokal »Lutter & Wegner« befand sich ebenfalls auf dem Gendarmenmarkt und seine Wohnung gleich nebenan in der Charlottenstraße, von wo er am 27. Juli 1817 mit ansehen musste, wie das Theater bis auf seine Grundmauern niederbrannte. Karl Friedrich Schinkel, der unter anderem auch die Kulissen für die »Zauberflöte« gestaltet hatte, wurde mit dem Neubau des Schauspielhauses beauftragt. Das nach seinen Plänen errichtete, 1821 eröffnete Gebäude verlieh dem Gendarmenmarkt die architektonische Vollkommenheit, die den Platz noch heute zu einem der schönsten Europas macht.

Café im Schatten der Bäume neben dem Französischen Dom auf dem Gendarmenmarkt.
Café in the shadow of the trees by the Französischer Dom (French Cathedral) in Gendarmenmarkt.

Die brennende Kuppel des Französischen Doms nach einem Luftangriff im Jahr 1943. Die Gebäude am Gendarmenmarkt wurden im Zweiten Weltkrieg stark zerstört und erst in den 1980er-Jahren wieder aufgebaut.
The dome of the Französischer Dom burning after an air raid in 1943. The buildings in Gendarmenmarkt were severely damaged in the Second World War and not rebuilt until the 1980s.

The story of Gendarmenmarkt started with the building of the French church in Friedrichstadt for the Berlin Huguenots and the German Lutheran church opposite around 1700; it had acquired its name under the Soldier King because the "Gens d'Armes" regiment had their stables here. Frederick the Great commissioned the architect Karl von Gontard to build the churches with their magnificent matching towers in 1780–85, and they were known as the French and German Cathedrals from then on. A "French Comedy House" was built between them, and under Friedrich Wilhelm II this became the "Royal National Theatre", gaining a new building in 1802. Lessing, Schiller and Goethe were per-

formed here, and so were Mozart's "Magic Flute" and E.T.A. Hoffmann's opera "Undine". E.T.A. Hoffmann's favourite wine bar "Lutter & Wegner" was also in Gendarmenmarkt; his home was in nearby Charlottenstrasse, from which he had to watch the theatre burn to the ground on 27 July 1817. Karl Friedrich Schinkel, who had designed the sets for the "Magic Flute" among other works, was commissioned to build the new Schauspielhaus. The building erected to his design and opened in 1821 gave Gendarmenmarkt the architectural perfection that still makes it one of the most beautiful squares in Europe today.

Das von Karl Friedrich Schinkel 1818–21 erbaute Schauspielhaus am Gendarmenmarkt ist heute das Konzerthaus Berlin; links der Deutsche Dom, Pendant zum gegenüberliegenden, hier nicht sichtbaren Französischen Dom.
The Schauspielhaus in Gendarmenmarkt was built by Karl Friedrich Schinkel in 1818–21, and is now Berlin's concert hall; on the left is the Deutscher Dom (German Cathedral), companion piece to the Französischer Dom (French Cathedral) opposite, which is not visible here.

Im Jahr 1851, zum 111. Jahrestag der Thronbesteigung Friedrichs II., des Großen, wurde das Denkmal des Preußenkönigs Unter den Linden enthüllt. Das dreizehneinhalb Meter hohe Reiterstandbild zählt zu den Hauptwerken des Bildhauers Christian Daniel Rauch. Den mittleren Teil des dreistufigen Postaments schmücken fast lebensgroße Darstellungen bedeutender Persönlichkeiten aus dem Umkreis des Monarchen und darüber befinden sich Reliefszenen aus dem Leben des Königs. An den Ecken symbolisieren Figuren die Herrschertugenden Weisheit, Mäßigung, Gerechtigkeit und Stärke. Nach dem Zweiten Weltkrieg wurde das Denkmal abgebaut, nach Potsdam verbracht, und erst Ende 1980 ließ es die DDR-Führung annähernd an seinem ursprünglichen Standort wieder aufstellen. Es markiert jene Stelle, an der der Herrscher einst mit dem Forum Fridericianum die Verschönerung der Umgebung des Stadtschlosses in Angriff nahm. Dazu gehörte auch das 1748–56 errichtete Palais nördlich der Linden, das er seinem Bruder Heinrich überließ. Im Prinz-Heinrich-Palais wurde dann 1810 die erste Berliner Universität eröffnet, an deren Gestaltung Wilhelm von Humboldt wesentlichen Anteil hatte.

The memorial to the Prussian king Frederick II, the Great, was unveiled in Unter den Linden in 1851, on the 111th anniversary of his accession to the throne. The equestrian statue is thirteen-and-a-half metres high and is a major work by the sculptor Christian Daniel Rauch. Almost life-size images of important figures from the monarch's entourage adorn the central section of the three-stepped pedestal, and above them are scenes from the king's life in relief. Figures at the corners symbolize the ruler's virtues of wisdom, moderation, justice and strength. The monument was demolished after the Second World War and taken to Potsdam. The GDR leadership did not allow it to be erected in approximately its original location until the late 1980s. It marks the place at which the ruler once started to beautify the area around the Stadtschloss with the Forum Fridericianum. This also included the palace built north of Unter den Linden in 1748–56, which he presented to his brother Heinrich. The first Berlin university was then opened in the Prinz-Heinrich-Palais in 1810, with Wilhelm von Humboldt significantly involved in its design.

Statue Alexander von Humboldts von Reinhold Begas vor der Universität. Zwei 1883 aufgestellte Denkmäler der Brüder Humboldt flankieren den Eingang zum Ehrenhof.
Statue of Alexander von Humboldt by Reinhold Begas outside the university. Two memorials to the Humboldt brothers erected in 1883 flank the entrance to the main courtyard.

Denkmal Friedrichs des Großen Unter den Linden, die Humboldt-Universität und
rechts die beleuchtete Fassade des Zeughauses.
*Unter den Linden monument to Frederick the Great, the Humboldt University
with the illuminated façade of the Zeughaus right.*

23

Die Königliche Bibliothek an der Westseite des Bebelplatzes, der einst das Zentrum des Forum Fridericianum bilden sollte, wurde 1775–80 nach Plänen von Georg Christian Unger durch Georg Friedrich Boumann den Jüngeren errichtet. In dem von den Berlinern wegen seiner geschwungenen Fassade »Kommode« genannten Gebäude waren bis zum Beginn des 20. Jahrhunderts die Bestände der Königlichen Bibliothek (später Staatsbibliothek) und im 19. Jahrhundert auch die der Friedrich-Wilhelms-Universität (diesen Namen trug die Berliner Universität 1828–1945) untergebracht. Heute befinden sich darin Räume der Humboldt-Universität.

Auf dem Bebelplatz – früher Opernplatz – fand am 10. Mai 1933 die Bücherverbrennung durch nationalsozialistische Studenten statt. Unter

Die ehemalige Königliche Bibliothek am Bebelplatz.
The former Royal Library in Bebelplatz.

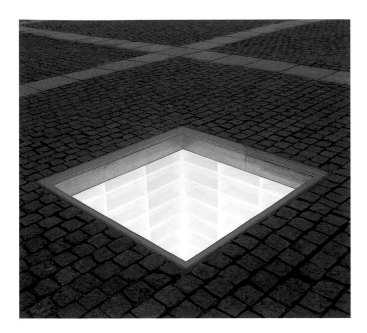

der Losung »Wider den undeutschen Geist« wurden hier über 20 000 Bücher von jüdischen, marxistischen und pazifistischen Autoren verbrannt. Im Gedenken an diesen Tag aus einem der dunkelsten Kapitel deutscher Geschichte errichtete der israelische Künstler Micha Ullman 1993–95 die unterirdische »Bibliothek«: versenkte leere Bücherregale, auf die man durch eine in den Boden gelassene Glasscheibe blickt.

The Royal Library on the west side of Bebelplatz, once intended as the centre of the Forum Fridericianum, was built in 1775–80 by Georg Friedrich Boumann the Younger to plans by Georg Christian Unger. The Berliner's called the building the "commode" because of its curved façade. Until the early 20th century it housed the Royal Library's holdings (later the State Library), and in the 19th century the Friedrich Wilhelm University's (Berlin University's name from 1828–1945) library as well. Its rooms are now used by the Humboldt University. National Socialist students burned books in Bebelplatz – formerly Opernplatz – on 10 May 1933. Over 20,000 books by Jewish, Marxist and pacifist authors went up in flames here, – because they were "Against the un-German spirit". The Israeli artist Micha Ullman built the underground "Library" from 1993–95 in memory of this day in the darkest chapter of German history: visitors see sunken empty bookcases viewed through a pane of glass let into the ground.

»Bibliothek«, Mahnmal zum Gedenken an die Bücherverbrennung auf dem Bebelplatz.
"Library", a monument in memory of the book-burning in Bebelplatz.

Bücherverbrennung durch die Nationalsozialisten am 10. Mai 1933 auf dem Opernplatz in Berlin.
The National Socialists burn books in Opernplatz in Berlin on 10 May 1933.

Nach den Befreiungskriegen von 1813, die mit der Niederlage Napoleons geendet hatten, beschloss Friedrich Wilhelm III., den Ausbau der »Linden« zur Prachtstraße fortzusetzen. Karl Friedrich Schinkel erhielt den Auftrag zur Errichtung einer neuen Königlichen Wache zwischen Zeughaus und Universität; er entwarf einen klar gegliederten Bau, der zu den gelungensten klassizistischen Bauwerken zählt. Auch das Areal ringsherum erhielt eine Verschönerungskur: Den übel riechenden Festungsgraben überdeckte man und legte ein Kastanienwäldchen an. Nach der Revolution von 1918 verlor das Gebäude seine Funktion und wurde 1931 zum Mahnmal für die Opfer des Ersten Weltkriegs umgestaltet. Die Nationalsozialisten widmeten es zum »Reichsehrenmal« um, weshalb die Sowjets nach 1945 zunächst den Abriss planten. 1960 jedoch weihte die DDR in der Schinkelschen Neuen Wache das Mahnmal für die Opfer des Faschismus und Militarismus ein. Nun flankierten Soldaten der Nationalen Volksarmee den Eingang und vollzogen regelmäßig im Stechschritt eine pompöse Wachablösung. Nach der »Wende«, 1993, erfolgte eine erneute Umgestaltung des Innenraums zur Gedenkstätte der Bundesrepublik für die Opfer von Krieg und Gewaltherrschaft.

After the Wars of Liberation in 1813, which had ended in the defeat of Napoleon, Friedrich Wilhelm III decided to continue extending the "Linden" as a show boulevard. Karl Friedrich Schinkel was commissioned to build a "Neue Wache" (new royal guardhouse) between the Zeughaus and the university; he designed a lucidly articulated structure that is considered to be one of the most successful neoclassical buildings. The surrounding area was smartened up as well: the evil-smelling fortification moat was covered over and a little chestnut wood planted. The building lost its function after the 1918 revolution and was redesigned as a memorial to the victims of the First World War in 1931. The National Socialists changed it into a "Reich Monument", which led the Soviets to contemplate pulling it down after 1945. But the GDR dedicated the Memorial to the Victims of Fascism and Militarism in Schinkel's Neue Wache in 1960. Now soldiers from the National People's Army flanked the entrance, regularly carrying out a grandiose changing of the guard in goose-step. After the fall of the Wall, in 1993, the interior was again redesigned as the National Memorial to the Victims of War and Tyranny.

Innenraum der Neuen Wache mit einer Plastik von Käthe Kollwitz.
Interior of the Neue Wache with a sculpture by Käthe Kollwitz.

Die im Zweiten Weltkrieg zerstörte Neue Wache im Juli 1945.
The Neue Wache in July 1945, severely damaged in the Second World War.

Die Neue Wache Unter den Linden, 1817/18 von Karl Friedrich Schinkel erbaut.
The Neue Wache in Unter den Linden, built in 1817/18 by Karl Friedrich Schinkel.

Erst unter Friedrich II. wurden die »Linden« zur Pracht- und Repräsentationsstraße der preußischen Residenz. Bei Regierungsantritt des Preußenkönigs im Jahr 1740 standen hier neben dem bereits 1706 fertig gestellten barocken Zeughaus, dem Kronprinzen- und dem Prinzessinnenpalais nur einfache Häuser der Hofbediensteten auf einem wüsten Gelände der einige Jahre zuvor eingeebneten Festungswälle und -gräben. Bereits im Mai 1740 erteilte Friedrich seinem Architekten Wenzeslaus von Knobelsdorff den Auftrag, vor den Fenstern des kronprinzlichen

Palais, am Sand- und Reitweg Unter den Linden, das Königliche Opernhaus zu errichten. Schon 1742 gab es hier erste Aufführungen und 1743 konnte das erste freistehende, vom Schloss unabhängige Opernhaus Deutschlands feierlich eingeweiht werden. 1786–88 erfolgte eine gründliche Modernisierung durch Carl Gotthard Langhans, den Erbauer des Brandenburger Tores. In den folgenden zwei Jahrhunderten erfuhr es mehrfache Umbauten und wurde nach der vollständigen Zerstörung im Zweiten Weltkrieg in den fünfziger Jahren wieder aufgebaut.

Blick vom Anfang der »Linden« auf das neue Königliche Opernhaus inmitten des noch kahlen ehemaligen Festungsgeländes, um 1745.
View from the beginning of the "Linden" of the new Royal Opera House in the midst of the still bleak fortress territory, c. 1745.

Statuen auf dem Dach des Opernhauses über der Fassade zum Bebelplatz.
Statues on the roof of the opera house above the Bebelplatz façade.

The "Linden" did not become the Prussian residence's show boulevard until the reign of Frederick II. On the Prussian king's accession in 1740 the only buildings here provided simple accommodation for court servants on the desolate terrain left after the fortified walls and moats had been demolished a few years before, alongside the baroque Zeughaus, completed as early as 1706, and the Kronprinzen- and Prinzessinnenpalais. Frederick commissioned his architect Wenzeslaus von Knobelsdorff to build the Royal Opera House in May 1740, outside the windows of the Kronprinzenpalais, on Unter den Linden, a sandy bridleway. The first performances were staged here as early as 1742, and the first free-standing opera house in Germany, independent of the palace, was solemnly opened in 1743. Carl Gotthard Langhans, who designed the Brandenburg Gate, modernized the building thoroughly in 1786–88. It was much modified over the next two centuries, and then rebuilt in the 1950s after being completely destroyed in the Second World War.

Die Deutsche Staatsoper Unter den Linden ist neben der Komischen Oper in der Behrenstraße und der Deutschen Oper in Charlottenburg eines der drei Opernhäuser Berlins.
Die Deutsche Staatsoper in Unter den Linden is one of Berlin's three opera houses, the others being the Komische Oper in Behrenstrasse and the Deutsche Oper in Charlottenburg.

Karl Friedrich Schinkel, der wohl berühmteste preußische Architekt, prägte vor allem mit seinen großartigen klassizistischen Bauten und der neugotischen Architektur das Berliner Stadtbild in der ersten Hälfte des 19. Jahrhunderts. Zunächst als Maler, Bühnenbildner, Innenarchitekt tätig, trat er durch die Förderung Wilhelm von Humboldts nach 1810 in den Dienst des staatlichen Bauwesens, wurde 1815 Geheimer Oberbaurat und später Oberlandesbaudirektor. Die Friedrichswerdersche Kirche entstand 1824–30 nach dem Vorbild gotischer »chapels« in England und war der erste neugotische Kirchenbau Berlins. Heute ist hier das Schinkelmuseum untergebracht. Östlich davon befand sich das 1832–36 nach Plänen Schinkels errichtete Gebäude der Bauakademie. Im Zweiten Weltkrieg zerstört, 1962 abgerissen, vermittelt heute eine hochgemauerte Ecke und eine Plastikfassade einen Eindruck vom wohlproportionierten Gebäude, für dessen Wiederaufbau Investoren gesucht werden. Zwischenzeitlich stand auf diesem Gelände das DDR-Außenministerium, das aber in neunziger Jahren abgerissen wurde.

Karl Friedrich Schinkel, probably the most famous Prussian architect, shaped the cityscape of Berlin in the first half of the 19th century, above all with his magnificent neo-classical buildings and neo-Gothic architecture. He first worked as a painter, set designer and interior designer, then moved into the state building service with the help of Wilhelm von Humboldt in 1810, achieving the high rank of Geheimer Oberbaurat in 1815, then becoming head of the department. The Friedrichswerdersche Kirche dates from 1824–30, and was modelled on English Gothic chapels. It was the first neo-Gothic church in Berlin, and now houses the Schinkel Museum. East of it was the Bauakademie, built to Schinkel's plans in 1832–36. This was destroyed in the Second World War, pulled down in 1962. Today a section of corner wall and a plastic façade convey an impression of this well-proportioned building. Developers are being sought for its reconstruction. In the meantime the GDR foreign ministry stood on this site, but it was pulled down in the 1990s.

Blick auf die Friedrichswerderschen Kirche 1959, rechts Schinkels Bauakademie.
View of the Friedrichswerdersche Kirche in 1959. On the right is Schinkel's Bauakademie.

Die Friedrichswerdersche Kirche Anfang der neunziger Jahre, rechts davon das inzwischen abgerissene DDR-Außenministerium.
The Friedrichswerdersche Kirche in the early nineties. On the right of it is the GDR Foreign Ministry, which has now been pulled down.

Die Friedrichswerdersche Kirche von Karl Friedrich Schinkel, im Vordergrund
die Statuen Schinkels (links, von Friedrich Drake) und des Agrarwissenschaftlers
Albrecht Thaer (rechts, von Christian Daniel Rauch).
Karl Friedrich Schinkel's Friedrichswerdersche Kirche, in the foreground are
statues of Schinkel (left, by Friedrich Drake) and the agrarian scientist Albrecht
Thaer (right, by Christian Daniel Rauch).

31

Vom 26. Januar bis 8. Mai 2005 war das Wort »Zweifel« auf dem Dach des
ehemaligen Palastes der Republik zu sehen. Die Installation des Künstlers Lars
Ramberg stand im Zusammenhang mit dessen virtueller Institution »Der Palast
des Zweifels«.
From 26 January to 8 May 2005 the word "Zweifel" (doubt) could be seen on
the roof of the former Palace of the Republic. This installation by the artist
Lars Ramberg was linked with his virtual institution "Palace of Doubt".

Nach der Sprengung des Berliner Stadtschlosses 1950/51 blieb der Marx-Engels-Platz (heute Schlossplatz) freies Gelände. Hier nahm die Partei- und Staatsführung der DDR die alljährlichen Paraden der Nationalen Volksarmee ab, und im Winter gab es den regelmäßig stattfindenden Ostberliner Weihnachtsmarkt. Als man begann, Ostberlin zur sozialistischen Hauptstadt der DDR auszubauen, entstand dort, wo der östliche Teil des Schlosses gestanden hatte, der Palast der Republik. Nach Plänen eines Kollektivs unter Heinz Graffunder wurde ein repräsentativer Bau aus Glas und Stahl mit dem Plenarsaal für die Volkskammer, einem Veranstaltungssaal mit über 4000 Sitzen, Restaurants, Cafés und Bars, einem Theater, einer Bowlingbahn und einem Jugendtreff errichtet. Der Palast entwickelte sich schnell zu einem beliebten Treffpunkt für DDR-Bürger – bis zu seiner Schließung am 19. September 1990 zählte man 70 Millionen Besucher. Nach der Asbestsanierung in den neunziger Jahren war nur noch der Rohbau übrig geblieben, in dem jedoch auf Initiative von Abrissgegnern zahlreiche attraktive Veranstaltungen stattgefunden haben – trotz des beschlossenen endgültigen Abrisses.

After the Berlin Stadtschloss was blown up in 1950/51 Marx-Engels-Platz (now Schlossplatz) was open terrain. Here the GDR party and state leadership took the salute at the annual parades of the National People's Army, and winter saw the regular East Berlin Christmas market. When East Berlin started to be built up as the socialist capital of the GDR, the Palace of the Republic was built on the site of the eastern section of the Stadtschloss. An imposing glass and steel building was erected to plans by a collective under Heinz Graffunder, housing a plenary chamber for the Volkskammer, an events hall seating over 4000, restaurants, cafés and bars, a theatre, a bowling alley and a young people's meeting-place. The palace rapidly became a popular rendezvous for all GDR citizens – 70 million visitors were counted before it closed on 19 September 1990. After asbestos had been removed in the nineties only the shell of the building remained, but numerous attractive events have taken place here on the initiative of people opposed to demolition – despite the fact that demolition has definitely been opted for.

Das aus einer mittelalterlichen Burganlage hervorgegangene Berliner Stadtschloss, das Friedrich I. von seinem Baumeister Andreas Schlüter Anfang des 18. Jahrhunderts errichten und umbauen ließ. Das Foto von 1903 zeigt im Vordergrund die Schlossbrücke und rechts die Bauten des 1897 eingeweihten Nationaldenkmals für Wilhelm I.
The Berlin Stadtschloss developed from a medieval fortress. Friedrich I commissioned the new Stadtschloss and modifications to the old palace from his master builder Andreas Schlüter in the early 18th century. This 1903 photograph shows the Schlossbrücke in the foreground and the National Monument to Wilhelm I, dedicated in 1897.

Blick vom Nordosten über die Kaiser-Wilhelm-Brücke (heute Liebknechtbrücke) zur Spreeseite des Stadtschlosses im Jahr 1904; an der rechten Ecke der so genannte Apothekenflügel. In dem von Rochus Graf zu Lynar 1580–95 für Kurfürst Johann Georg errichteten Flügel war die Hofapotheke untergebracht.
View from the north-east over the Kaiser-Wilhelm-Brücke (now Liebknecht-Brücke) towards the Spree side of the Stadtschloss in 1904; at the right-hand corner is the so-called Apothekenflügel. The court apothecary's shop was housed in this wing, built by Rochus Graf zu Lynar in 1580–95 for Elector Johann Georg.

Auf dem Areal zu Füßen des Fernsehturms, wo sich die Marienkirche aus dem 13. Jahrhundert wie eine vergessene Preziose ausnimmt, befanden sich bis ins 20. Jahrhundert Häuser – dicht gedrängt und verbunden durch ein umfangreiches Straßennetz. Das Viertel wurde im Zweiten Weltkrieg weitgehend zerstört und später abgetragen. In den achtziger Jahren wandelte man die Freifläche hinter dem Neptunbrunnen zur Spree hin zum Marx-Engels-Forum um; am 4. April 1986, dem Vorabend des 11. Parteitags der SED, wurde es feierlich eingeweiht. Die Anlage des Forums gestaltete der Bildhauer Ludwig Engelhart mit einem Künstlerkollektiv. Innerhalb einer zentralen Kreisfläche von etwa 60 Metern Durchmesser erheben sich die überlebensgroßen Bronze-

Blick vom Roten Rathaus in Richtung Westen mit dem Stadtschloss (hinten links) und dem Dom im Jahr 1922. Im Vordergrund die Bebauung auf dem Areal des heutigen Marx-Engels-Forums.
View from the Rotes Rathaus looking west with the Stadtschloss (left) and the Berliner Dom in 1922. The site of the present Marx-Engels Forum is being developed in the foreground.

figuren der Begründer des wissenschaftlichen Sozialismus. Außerhalb des Kreises wurden unter anderem eine Marmorrelief-Wand von Werner Stötzer aufgestellt, deren Darstellungen die »unmenschlichen kapitalistischen Zustände der alten kapitalistischen Welt« versinnbildlichen, sowie zwei Bronze-Reliefs von Margret Middell mit Szenen aus dem Leben einer »befreiten Gesellschaft«.

Until well into the 20th century there used to be houses in the area at the foot of the Television Tower where the 13th century Marienkirche stands like a forgotten, precious thing. The houses were packed tightly together, and linked by an extensive network of streets. The quarter

was largely destroyed in the Second World War, and later demolished. In the eighties, the resultant open space behind the Neptune fountain on the Spree side was transformed into the Marx-Engels-Forum; it was solemnly opened on 4 April 1986, the day before the SED's 11th party conference. The Forum facilities were designed by the sculptor Ludwig Engelhart, working with an artists' collective. Larger-than-life statues of the founders of scientific socialism tower up inside a circular central area about 60m in diameter. Features outside the circle included a relief wall by Werner Stötzer, with depictions symbolizing "inhuman capitalist conditions in the old capitalist world," and two bronze reliefs by Margret Middell with scenes from the life of a "liberated society".

Die Plastik des Bildhauers Ludwig Engelhart bildet den zentralen Punkt des Marx-Engels-Forums; im Hintergrund, jenseits der Spree, die Fassade vom ehemaligen Palast der Republik.
This sculpture by Ludwig Engelhart used to provide a focus for the Marx-Engels-Forum. In the background, on the other side of the Spree, is the façade of the former Palace of the Republic.

Seit 1986 scheinen Karl Marx und Friedrich Engels hier auf den Fernsehturm zu blicken, den Rücken dem Palast der Republik zugedreht.
Since 1986, Marx and Engels have seemed to be looking at the Television Tower, turning their backs on the Palace of the Republic.

35

NIKOLAIVIERTEL

Das Nikolaiviertel bedeckt heute ein Gebiet, auf dem Berlin vor etwa 800 Jahren entstanden ist. 1230 schon gab es Vorgängerbauten der Nikolaikirche und 1470 errichtete man nach einem Brand die Kirche in ihrer heutigen Gestalt. Von den beiden vorgesehenen Türmen existierte bis ins 19. Jahrhundert allerdings nur einer, 1878 hatte man dann offenbar die Mittel für das sich in den Himmel reckende gotische Turmpaar. Nach dem Zweiten Weltkrieg war die Kirche zerstört, und die Umgebung lag in Trümmern, die man später beseitigte. Erst im Rahmen der Vorbereitungen auf das 750-jährige Jubiläum Berlins 1987 rückte das Gebiet ins Blickfeld der Stadtplaner. Die Hauptstadt der DDR sollte zu dem denkwürdigen Anlass hier wieder eine Altstadt bekommen. Die Kirche wurde erneuert und ringsherum errichtete man entsprechend dem überlieferten Straßenraster Altberliner Bürgerhäuser und Plattenbauten mit historischem Ambiente. Berühmte Gebäude aus der Geschichte Berlins wie die Gerichtslaube, das Ephraimpalais oder das Restaurant »Nussbaum« erhielten im Nikolaiviertel eine neue Heimat.

The Nikolaiviertel now covers an area that Berlin used to occupy about 800 years ago. Predecessor buildings to the Nikolaikirche existed as early as 1230, and the church was built in its present form in 1470, after a fire. Until the 19th century only one of the two planned towers existed, but by 1878 its seems that sufficient funds had accumulated for the soaring pair of Gothic towers. The church was in ruins after the Second World War and the surrounding area was reduced to rubble, which was later removed. The site did not shift into the town planners' field of vision until preparations started for Berlin's 750th anniversary in 1987. The capital of the GDR was to acquire an old town again for this memorable occasion. The church was rebuilt from scratch, and Old Berlin town houses and slab constructions with a historical aura were built all around it on the former street grid. Famous buildings from Berlin history like the Gerichtslaube, a court formerly attached to the town hall, the Ephraimpalais or the "Nussbaum" restaurant found a new home in the Nikolaiviertel.

Nach historischen Vorbildern wurden die Bürgerhäuser gegenüber der Nikolaikirche errichtet.
The town houses opposite the Nikolaikirche were built following historical models.

Anfang der siebziger Jahren war die Ruine der im Zweiten Weltkrieg zerstörten Nikolaikirche (hinter dem Roten Rathaus) noch von einer Brache umgeben.
In the early seventies the ruins of the Nikolaikirche (behind the Rotes Rathaus), severely damaged in the Second World War, were still surrounded by derelict land.

Die Nikolaikirche, das älteste Bauwerk Berlins, steht inmitten des Nikolaiviertels.
The Nicolaikirche, Berlin's oldest building, is in the middle of the Nikolaiviertel.

Der Westberliner Senat war in den Jahren der Teilung seit 1949 zu Gast im Rathaus Schöneberg. Einen gemeinsamen Senat gibt es wieder seit den ersten Gesamtberliner Wahlen, die nach dem Mauerfall stattfanden. Mit dem Regierenden Bürgermeister zog die Regierung für ganz Berlin im Oktober 1991 wieder an den traditionsreichen Ort.

The monumental Rotes Rathaus (Red Town Hall) rises on the site where the Berlin town hall stood as early as the 13th century. The Berlin municipal authority had its first meeting here in 1865, and the councillors' assembly met here from 1870. As Berlin grew enormously in the late 19th century there was not enough room for the administration after a very few decades, so the Neues Stadthaus was built in Molkenmarkt in 1902–11. The Rotes Rathaus was badly damaged in the Second World War. Until it was rebuilt, the East Berlin city authority was based first in the Stadthaus after the division of Berlin, and then moved back into the Rotes Rathaus from 1955, after rebuilding work was completed. The West Berlin Senate has been a guest in Schöneberg Town Hall since the division in 1949. There has been a joint Senate only since the first elections for the whole of Berlin, which took place after the Wall fell. The governing mayor and the government of all Berlin moved back into this location, so rich in tradition, in October 1991.

An dem Ort, wo schon Mitte des 13. Jahrhunderts das Rathaus der Berliner gestanden hat, erhebt sich heute der monumentale Bau des Roten Rathauses. 1865 hielt der Berliner Magistrat hier seine erste Sitzung ab und 1870 die Stadtverordnetenversammlung. Mit dem enormen Wachstum Berlins Ende des 19. Jahrhunderts reichte auch der Platz für die Verwaltung nach wenigen Jahrzehnten nicht mehr aus, sodass 1902–11 zusätzlich das Neue Stadthaus am Molkenmarkt entstand. Im Zweiten Weltkrieg wurde das Rote Rathaus stark zerstört. Bis zu seinem Wiederaufbau residierte nach der Spaltung Berlins der Ostberliner Magistrat zunächst im Stadthaus und nach dem Abschluss der Wiederaufbauarbeiten ab 1955 wieder im Roten Rathaus.

Neptun vis-à-vis vom Roten Rathaus. Der heute im Schatten des Fernsehturms stehende Neptunbrunnen, geschaffen 1886–91 von Reinhold Begas, hatte seinen Standort ursprünglich gegenüber vom Schloss.
Neptune opposite the Rotes Rathaus. The Neptune fountain, now in the shadow of the Television Tower, was created in 1886–91 by Reinhold Begas. It was originally sited opposite the Stadtschloss.

Der Schlossplatz mit dem Neptunbrunnen um 1900, links die Südfront des Schlosses, im Hintergrund die Rathausstraße und der Turm des Roten Rathauses.
Schlossplatz with the Neptune Fountain around 1900. On the left is the south façade of the Schloss, in the background Rathausstrasse and the tower of the Rotes Rathaus.

Das 1861–69 errichtete Rote Rathaus – so benannt nach den roten Klinker-
steinen – ist Sitz des Regierenden Bürgermeisters und des Berliner Senats.
The Rotes Rathaus – so-called because of its red brick – is the seat of the
governing mayor and the Berlin Senate.

Blick vom Lustgarten auf den Berliner Dom, rechts der Fernsehturm am Alexanderplatz.
View from the Lustgarten of the Berlin Cathedral, on the right is the Television Tower in Alexanderplatz.

GUARDIAN NOV 29th '08

International

From PRUSSIAN PALACE to

From people's palace back to Prussian palace

Kaiser's residence to be rebuilt on east Berlin site

Communist-era building finally swept away

Kate Connolly Berlin

A jury of artists, politicians and city planners voted in favour of the reconstruction of a Prussian palace in Berlin yesterday, just as the last remnants of the East German parliament building on the site were being dragged away.

But the plan to reinstate the last residence of Kaiser Wilhelm II has been hotly disputed between those who wanted a new architectural centrepiece for east Berlin and those nostalgic for the communist-era palace where they celebrated their coming of age parties or went bowling.

As the decision was being announced, a single remaining staircase of the once colossal Palace of the Republic was sticking out of the ground like a jagged tooth. Onlookers with cameras captured the moment it was prised from its moorings by a hydraulic digger.

Yesterday an Italian architectural firm, Francesco Stella, beat 39 other architects to win the contract to replace it with a re-creation of the 18th century Prussian palace, which was destroyed by second world war bombing. Communist authorities swept away all traces of the baroque building in the 1950s, replacing it with their own version of a people's palace

The last vestiges of east Berlin's Palace of the Republic are torn down Photograph: Theo Heimann/AFP/Getty

— a glass-fronted eyesore that served as a parliament headquarters and a recreation centre.

In 1990, after the fall of the Berlin wall, the building was deemed unsafe and was closed. Almost 80,000 tonnes of asbestos were removed before it was painstakingly dismantled over three years.

"It wasn't an easy decision," said the construction minister, Wolfgang Tiefensee, himself an easterner. "It's such a sensitive building and there's so much history. But the decision we've made is anything but a lousy compromise."

suspected an establishment plot to snuff out all traces of the communist era. If the palace had to go, could it not have been replaced by a less ideologically driven post-Prussian central park instead? one critic asked. But city planners ignored critics who said the €552m (£456m) project was an attempt to "whitewash" history and an insult to modern-day architecture.

Yesterday the jury praised Stella's design as a "clever architectural connection of old and new, of modern usage and the reconstruction of the former palace".

He will have to reconstruct three of

last ornament, curlicue and naked angel, allowing little freedom for personal interpretation. Even the head of the jury, Italian architect Vittorio Lampugnani, criticised the aesthetics of the project, saying he was "against the claim that the old palace would be the best thing to put here".

But a lobby group supported by much of the political elite won out, arguing that going back to a Prussian design would help to heal the wounds still felt since reunification 18 years ago. Construction of the palace, which will house an art collection and an entertainment and hotel complex,

their last hundred million but
elite still enjoy fun of the fair

Im Auftrag von Wilhelm II. entstand zwischen 1894 und 1905 der Berliner Dom nach Plänen von Julius Carl Raschdorff. Der Vorgängerbau, im 18. Jahrhundert errichtet und 1822 von Schinkel umgestaltet, erschien dem Kaiser zu bescheiden, und so wünschte er sich für seine evangelische Staatskirche ein repräsentativeres Gotteshaus. Mit dem Wiederaufbau des im Zweiten Weltkrieg stark zerstörten Gebäudes wurde 1975 begonnen, dabei erfuhr vor allem die Kuppel entscheidende Veränderungen. Die Wiederherstellung des Inneren nahm Jahrzehnte in Anspruch; seit 1999 ist die Hohenzollerngruft u. a. mit den Sarkophagen des Großen Kurfürsten, König Friedrichs I. und des Soldatenkönigs wieder zugänglich. Ein repräsentatives Bauwerk wünschte sich seinerzeit auch der DDR-Staatsratsvorsitzende Walter Ulbricht und ließ deshalb – als Pendant zum Palast der Republik – den Fernsehturm inmitten der »Hauptstadt der DDR« errichten. Im Oktober 1969 wurde er in Betrieb genommen und ist noch heute mit seiner Aussichtsplattform und dem drehbaren Telecafé in über 200 Metern Höhe eine Touristenattraktion.

Wilhelm II commissioned the Berlin Cathedral, and it was built to plans Julius Carl Raschdorff between 1894 and 1905. The earlier building, built in the 18th century and redesigned by Schinkel in 1822, seemed too modest to the Kaiser, so he asked for a more imposing edifice for his Protestant state church. Work on rebuilding the church, which was badly damaged in the Second World War, started in 1975, with the dome in particular undergoing major changes. Restoring the interior took decades; the Hohenzollern vault, containing sarcophaguses for the Great Elector, King Frederick I and the Soldier King among others, is now open again. The GDR Party Chairman Walter Ulbricht wanted an imposing building for himself too, and so had the Television Tower built in the middle of the "GDR capital" – as a companion piece to the Palace of the Republic. It started operating in October 1969, and is still a tourist attraction today with its viewing platform and revolving Telecafé at over 200 metres.

Mit seiner beträchtlichen Höhe von 368 Metern überragt der Fernsehturm die Kuppel des Doms, von der man allerdings in einer Höhe von 50 Metern ebenfalls eine herrliche Rundumsicht genießen kann.
At a considerable height of 368 metres the Television Tower rises above the Cathedral dome, though the latter also affords a splendid panorama from a height of 50 metres.

Der Plan Friedrich Wilhelms III., die königlichen Gemäldesammlungen der Öffentlichkeit zugänglich zu machen, gab den Anstoß für die Errichtung des ersten, eigenständigen Museumsgebäudes in Berlin. Den Bauplatz gegenüber vom Schloss gewann man durch das Zuschütten eines Kanals an dieser Stelle. Karl Friedrich Schinkel entwarf 1822 einen zweistöckigen, geschlossenen Bau mit einem durch beide Geschosse reichenden Kuppelsaal, der sich zur Säulenhalle und zur großen Freitreppe zum Lustgarten hin öffnet. Vor dem 1830 fertig gestellten Gebäude, das inzwischen zu den berühmtesten klassizistischen Bauwerken gehört, plante Schinkel die Aufstellung einer Granitschale. Sie hat einen Durchmesser von fast sieben Metern und wiegt knapp 80 Tonnen. Der Steinmetzmeister Gottlieb Christian Cantian hat sie aus einem Findling aus den Rauenschen Bergen gearbeitet, für dessen Transport auf dem Wasser aus der Gegend bei Fürstenwalde extra ein Schiff gebaut werden musste.

King Friedrich Wilhelm III's plan to open the royal painting collection to the public prompted the building of Berlin's first independent museum. The site opposite the Stadtschloss was created by filling in a canal at this point. Karl Friedrich Schinkel designed a two-storey, unified building with a domed hall rising through two storeys, opening on to the portico and the large broad flight of open steps down to the Lustgarten.

Winterlicher Spätnachmittag im Lustgarten.
Late winter afternoon in the Lustgarten.

Von oben gesehen: der Lustgarten mit dem Alten Museum auf der Spreeinsel; links der Kupfergraben, rechts hinter dem Dom die Spree.
Seen from above: the Lustgarten with the Altes Museum on the Spree Island; on the left is the Kupfergraben, on the right, behind the Berlin Cathedral, is the Spree.

Die als biedermeierliches Weltwunder bestaunte Granitschale im Lustgarten, links der alte Dom und hinten das Schloss; Gemälde von Johann Erdmann Hummel aus dem Jahr 1831.
The granite bowl in the Lustgarten, marvelled at as a wonder of the Biedermeier world; on the left is the old cathedral and behind it the Stadtschloss. Painting by Johann Erdmann Hummel dating from 1831.

The museum was completed in 1830, and is now one of the most famous neoclassical buildings. Schinkel planned to set up a granite bowl
in front of it, almost seven metres in diameter, and weighing just under
80 tons. The master mason Gottlieb Christian Cantian carved it from an
erratic block found in the Rauen hills. A boat had to be built specially to
transport it from the area near Fürstenwalde by water.

Die ionische Säulenhalle des Alten Museums an der Nordseite des Lustgartens.
The Ionic colonnade of the Altes Museum on the north side of the Lustgarten.

Der tempelartige Bau der Alten Nationalgalerie war Teil des Planes, den Friedrich Wilhelm IV. und sein Baumeister Friedrich August Stüler für die Bebauung der Spreeinsel vorgesehen hatten. Nach dem Tod von Stüler 1866 – der König war bereits 1861 gestorben – wurde dieser dritte Bau auf dem Areal an der Spree von Karl Heinz Strack ausgeführt, und mit der nationalen Einigungsbewegung entschloss man sich, hier ein Museum der deutschen Kunst einzurichten. Obwohl das Haus erst 1876 eingeweiht wurde, prangt über den Säulen in goldenen Lettern »Der deutschen Kunst 1871« im Gedenken an die Gründung des Deutschen Kaiserreichs im Jahr 1871. Nach diesem Datum löste der Begriff »Museumsinsel« auch langsam den Begriff »Spreeinsel« ab. Die Zerstörungen, die das Gebäude im Zweiten Weltkrieg erlitt, konnten bis 1955 beseitigt werden, eine tiefgreifende Restaurierung erfuhr die Alte Nationalgalerie dann Ende der neunziger Jahre. Seit ihrer Wiedereröffnung im Jahr 2001 ist hier die Kunst des 19. Jahrhunderts zu sehen.

The temple-like building for the Alte Nationalgalerie was part of the plan devised by Friedrich Wilhelm IV and his architect Friedrich August

Stüler for developing the Spree Island. After Stüler died in 1866 – the king had already died in 1861 – this third building was realized by Karl Heinz Strack on the site by the Spree, and the spirit of the German unification movement suggested setting up a museum of German art here. Even though the building was not opened until 1876, the inscription "Der deutschen Kunst 1871" ("To German art 1871") is resplendent in

Umgeben von offenen Kolonnadengängen erhebt sich die Alte Nationalgalerie wie ein korinthischer Tempel an der Spree; links das Neue Museum, Fotografie um 1900.
The Alte Nationalgalerie soars up like a Corinthian temple on the Spree, surrounded by open colonnades; photograph c. 1900.

Freiluftkino vor der Alten Nationalgalerie.
Open-air cinema in front of the Alte Nationalgalerie.

gold letters above the columns, in memory of the foundation of the
German Reich in 1871. After this date the term "Spree Island" was also
gradually replaced by "Museum Island". The damage suffered by the
building in the Second World War was made good by 1955, and the
Alte Nationalgalerie was then thoroughly restored in the late nineties.
19th century art has been shown here since it reopened in 2001.

Die Alte Nationalgalerie auf der Museumsinsel mit dem Reiterstandbild des
Gründers Friedrich Wilhelm IV; 1886 nach einem Entwurf Gustav Blaesers aufgestellt.
*The Alte Nationalgalerie on the Museum Island with the equestrian statue of
the founder, Friedrich Wilhelm IV, set up in 1886 to a design by Gustav Blaeser.*

Schon 1823 wurde die Sammlung Ägyptischer Kunst in Berlin gegründet, 1850 erhielt sie im Neuen Museum ein ihr gebührendes Domizil. Entsprechend der Idee Friedrich Wilhelms IV., auf der Spreeinsel einen Komplex mit Bauten der Kunst und Wissenschaft zu errichten, schuf Friedrich August Stüler als zweites Gebäude nach dem Schinkelschen Alten Museum 1843–45 das Neue Museum. Beide Häuser waren einstmals durch einen auf einem Bogen ruhenden Gang miteinander verbunden. Die Kolonnaden an der Süd- und Ostseite umschlossen den Gartenhof, in den nach Stülers Plänen nach 1860 die Nationalgalerie gesetzt wurde. Das Neue Museum mit seinen prächtig ausgestalteten Innenräumen erlitt im Zweiten Weltkrieg große Schäden; mit seinem Wiederaufbau ist erst in den neunziger Jahren begonnen worden.

Über vier Jahrzehnte gab es in der geteilten Stadt zwei Ägyptische Museen: im Bode-Museum in Ostberlin und im Stülerbau gegenüber dem Schloss Charlottenburg in Westberlin. Bis das Neue Museum im Jahr 2009 wiedereröffnet werden kann, hat die wieder vereinte Sammlung Ägyptischer Kunst ihren Platz im Obergeschoss des Alten Museums.

The Egyptian Art Collection was established in Berlin as early as 1823, and it acquired a home worthy of its status in the Neues Museum in 1850. Following Friedrich Wilhelm IV's idea of putting up a complex of art and science buildings on the Spree Island, Friedrich August Stüler designed and built the Neues Museum in 1843–45 as the second building after Schinkel's Altes Museum. The two museums used to be

Blick in einen Ausstellungsraum des Ägyptischen Museums.
View into an exhibition gallery in the Egyptian Museum.

Das prunkvolle Haupttreppenhaus des Neuen Museums auf einem Aquarell von 1910.
The magnificent main staircase of the Neues Museum in a 1910 water colour.

connected by a passageway resting on an arch. The colonnades on the
south and east sides surrounded the garden court, and the Nationalgalerie was placed here to Stüler's plans after 1860. The Neues Museum
with its magnificently designed interiors suffered considerable damage
in the Second World War; rebuilding work did not start until the 1990s.
There were two Egyptian museums in the divided city for four decades:
in the Bode-Museum in East Berlin and in the Stüler building opposite
Schloss Charlottenburg in West Berlin. The Egyptian collection has now
been reunited and is housed on the top floor of the Altes Museum until
the Neues Museum reopens in 2009.

Die über 3000 Jahre alte Büste der Königin Nofretete ist ein Highlight des
Ägyptischen Museums.
The bust of Queen Nefertiti is over 3000 years old and a highlight of the
Egyptian Museum.

lichen Probleme verzögerte. Erst 1930 konnte der monumentale Bau – der letzte auf der Museumsinsel – eingeweiht werden. Heute beherbergt das Pergamonmuseum im Nordflügel die Antikensammlung mit den Architektursälen und dem Skulpturentrakt, das Vorderasiatische Museum und das Museum für Islamische Kunst.

In the late 19th and early 20th century, when archaeological excavations were really booming in Greece and the Middle East, room for the art treasures found there soon became scarce in the existing Berlin institutions. There was pressure to create a new building, so that the public could see the results of all this archaeological work as well. A building for the most important excavation finds went up north of the Neues Museum in 1901, but it soon turned out to be too small and too light for exhibits like the Pergamon Frieze. The architect Alfred Messel started to design the Pergamon Museum in 1907, but its completion under Ludwig Hoffmann was delayed by the First World War and the subsequent economic problems. The monumental building – the last on the Museum Island – was not finally opened until 1930. Today the north wing of the Pergamon Museum contains the antiquities collection with architecture galleries and the sculpture section, the Museum of the Middle East and the Museum of Islamic Art.

Als Ende des 19./Anfang des 20. Jahrhunderts die archäologischen Ausgrabungen in Griechenland und im vorderasiatischen Raum einen wahren Boom erlebten, wurde der Platz für die geborgenen Kunstschätze in den bestehenden Berliner Instituten bald knapp. Man drängte auf einen Neubau, um die Ergebnisse der archäologischen Arbeit auch der Öffentlichkeit zeigen zu können. 1901 entstand nördlich des Neuen Museums ein Bau für die bedeutendsten Ausgrabungsfunde, doch erwies er sich bald als zu klein und zu leicht für Exponate wie den Pergamonfries. 1907 begann der Architekt Alfred Messel mit den Entwürfen für das Pergamonmuseum, dessen Fertigstellung unter Ludwig Hoffmann sich jedoch durch den Ersten Weltkrieg und die nachfolgenden wirtschaft-

Die Bahntrasse zwischen den S-Bahnhöfen Friedrichstraße und Hackescher Markt trennt das Pergamonmuseum im Süden der Museumsinsel vom Bode-Museum an der Nordspitze.
The railway line between Friedrichstrasse and Hackescher Markt S-Bahn stations divides the Pergamon Museum in the south of the Museum Island from the Bode-Museum on the northern tip.

Der durch Bombenangriffe im Zweiten Weltkrieg zerstörte Saal für den Pergamonaltar.
The gallery for the Pergamon Altar, destroyed by air raids in the Second World War.

Babylons Ischtar-Tor aus dem 6. Jahrhundert v. Chr. im Vorderasiatischen Museum, das sich im Gebäude des Pergamonmuseums befindet.
Babylon's Ishtar Gate, dating from the 6th century BC, in the Museum of the Middle East, which is housed in the Pergamon Museum building.

Die Hackeschen Höfe mit ihren Cafés, Restaurants, Geschäften, Galerien und
Theatern gehören zu den lebendigsten Orten der Stadt.
*The Hackesche Höfe with their cafés, restaurants, shops, galleries and theatres
are among the city's liveliest locations.*

Die Straßen und Plätze um den Hackeschen Markt in Berlin-Mitte gehörten einst zur Spandauer Vorstadt, eine Stadterweiterung, deren
Ausgangspunkt der sich um 1750 herausbildende Hackesche Markt war
– benannt nach Johann Christoph Friedrich Graf von Hacke, der damals
hier die Neubebauung leitete. Ursprünglich war es ein Platz vor dem
mittelalterlichen Spandauer Tor, wo mehrere Straßen aus dem Norden
zusammenkamen. In der neuen Vorstadt ließen sich viele Gewerbetrei-
bende nieder, die auch in dem Viertel ihr Zuhause hatten. Mit den Ände-
rungen der Wirtschaftsstrukturen Anfang des 19. Jahrhunderts verarm-
ten viele von ihnen und so veränderte sich auch der Charakter der
Gegend – im 19. Jahrhundert hatte die Spandauer Vorstadt den Ruf, ein
Ort der Diebe und der leichten Mädchen zu sein. Mit dem Wirtschafts-
boom in der kaiserlichen Hauptstadt nach 1870 siedelten sich jedoch
wieder neue Unternehmen an, ein Großteil der alten Häuser wurde
abgerissen und durch neue, vierstöckige Häuser mit Gewerbehöfen
ersetzt. Die Hackeschen Höfe entstanden 1906/07 nach Plänen des
Jugendstilarchitekten August Endell. Er entwarf schon damals die
heute so anziehende Mischung zwischen Wohnen, Festsälen, Klubs
und Gewerbe.

*The streets and squares around the Hackescher Markt in the Mitte dis-
trict of Berlin were once part of the Spandauer Vorstadt, an extension
to the city that started around the Hackescher Markt, which came into
being in about 1750. The market was named after Christoph Friedrich
Graf von Hacke, who was in charge of the new building programme at
the time. Originally it was a square in front of the medieval Spandauer
Tor, where several roads coming from the north joined. A large number
of tradespeople settled in the new quarter and made their homes there.
Changes in the economic structure in the early 19th century meant that
many of them fell into poverty, and so the character of the area also
changed – in the 19th century the Spandauer Vorstadt had the reputation of being a haunt of thieves and women of easy virtue. But the economic boom in the imperial city in the 1870s brought new businesses
into the area again, and the majority of the old houses were replaced
by new, four-storey buildings with commercial yards. The Hackesche
Höfe were built in 1906/07 to plans by the Jugendstil architect August
Endell. Even then he designed the mixture that is so popular today of
housing, dance halls, clubs and commerce.*

Blick vom Hackeschen Markt in die Oranienburger Straße.
View from the Hackescher Markt into Oranienburger Strasse.

Die 1995–97 sanierten Hackeschen Höfe, rechts führt die Rosenthaler Straße in
Richtung Norden.
*View of the Hackesche Höfe, refurbished in 1995–97. Rosenthaler Strasse, on
the right, runs in a northerly direction.*

Aussicht von einem Wohnhaus in der Rochstraße auf den S-Bahnhof Hackescher Markt und das angrenzende Scheunenviertel mit den Hackeschen Höfen auf der rechten Seite.
The view from an apartment building on Rochstrasse over the Hackescher Markt S-Bahn station and the neighbouring quarter Scheunenviertel, with the court-yard complex of the Hackesche Höfe on the right-hand side.

Gruss aus Berlin.

Synagoge in der Oranienburgerstras

Fünfzig Jahre nach dem Ende des nationalsozialistischen Terrors konnte am 7. Mai 1995 die Neue Synagoge in der Oranienburger Straße zum zweiten Mal eingeweiht werden. Schon 1859 hatte man mit ihrem Bau nach Entwürfen von Eduard Knoblauch und Friedrich August Stüler begonnen, und am 5. September 1866 war sie den Gläubigen übergeben worden. Mit über 3000 Sitzplätzen galt sie als das größte und prächtigste jüdische Gotteshaus Deutschlands und zugleich als Ausdruck eines selbstbewussten, etablierten jüdischen Bürgertums in der Stadt. In der Pogromnacht am 9. November 1938 steckten Nationalsozialisten das Gebäude in Brand, aber durch die Zivilcourage eines verantwortlichen Polizisten konnte größerer Schaden abgewendet werden. Bei einem Bombenangriff am 23. November 1943 wurde das Haus jedoch dann endgültig zerstört; die Hauptsynagoge sprengte man daher im Jahr 1958. Dreißig Jahre später beschloss man, die noch existierende Ruine des zur Straße gelegenen Teils mit Rotunde, Vestibül, Ausstellungs- und Vortragssaal wieder aufzubauen. Darin befindet sich heute das für jeden zugängliche Centrum Judaicum. Im Hof markieren schwarze Granitsteine die Apsis des nicht wieder errichteten Haupthauses.

On 7 May 1995, fifty years after the end of the National Socialist terror, the New Synagogue in Oranienburger Strasse was consecrated for the second time. Work started on building it as early as 1859, to designs by Eduard Knoblauch and Friedrich August Stüler, and it was handed over to the faithful on 5 September 1866. It seated over 3000 people, and

Die golden leuchtende Kuppel der Synagoge überragt die Alt-Berliner Straßenzüge zwischen dem Hackeschen Markt und der Friedrichstraße.
The synagogue dome, gleaming in gold, rises over the streets of Old Berlin between the Hackescher Markt and Friedrichstrasse.

Die Neue Synagoge auf einer Ansichtspostkarte aus dem Jahr 1900.
A 1900 postcard of the New Synagogue.

was considered to be one of the largest and most magnificent Jewish houses of God in Germany, and at the same time expressing the confident, established presence of Jewish citizens in the city.
On 9 November 1938, the night of the pogrom, National Socialists set the building on fire, but a single policeman showing the courage of his convictions prevented major damage. But the building was finally de-stroyed in an air raid on 23 November 1943, and its remains were blown up in 1958. The decision was taken thirty years later to rebuild the surviving ruins on the street side, including the rotunda, vestibule, exhibition- and lecture-hall. It now houses the Centrum Judaicum, which is open to all. Black granite stones in the courtyard mark the apse of the main building, which was not reconstructed.

In 50 Meter Höhe erhebt sich der Davidstern über den Kuppeln der Neuen Synagoge in der Oranienburger Straße.
The Star of David soars 50 metres above the domes of the New Synagogue in Oranienburger Strasse.

Einst waren sie Anziehungspunkt für die Bewohner der Spandauer Vorstadt: die Friedrichstraßen-Passagen. Zu Beginn des 20. Jahrhunderts entstanden sie auf dem Eckgrundstück Friedrichstraße/Oranienburger Straße in dem unter der Leitung des Architekten Franz Ahrens 1907–09 errichteten Passage-Kaufhaus. Dessen Attraktivität sank allerdings nach dem Ersten Weltkrieg, 1928 wurde deshalb daraus das »Haus der Technik«, ein Repräsentationsgebäude der AEG. Nach dem Zweiten Weltkrieg baute man den von Bomben stark zerstörten Baukomplex nie wieder richtig auf, nur einige Geschäfte zogen ein und ein Filmtheater, das als Kino des Staatlichen Filmarchivs unter dem Namen »Camera« zum Anziehungspunkt der Cineasten in Ostberlin wurde. Im Jahr nach dem Fall der Mauer besetzten Künstler die Ruine und kamen so einem Abriss zuvor. Es entstanden Ateliers, Ausstellungsräume, Szenecafés und auch wieder ein Kino. Inzwischen ist das »Tacheles«, wie die Künstler ihr Haus nannten, zu einer Attraktion der Stadt Berlin geworden.

The Friedrichstrasse arcades, once a draw for the residents of the Spandauer Vorstadt. They came into being in the early 20th century on the plot at the corner of Friedrichstrasse and Oranienburger Strasse in the Passage department store built under the direction of the architect Franz Ahrens in 1907–09. They became less attractive after the First World War, however, and so in 1928 they were incorporated into the "Haus der Technik", a prestigious building for AEG. After the Second World War the building complex, which had been badly damaged in air raids, was never properly rebuilt. There were just a few shops to bring people in, and a cinema used by the State Film Archive. It was called "Camera", and popular with East Berlin film fans. Artists occupied the ruins in the year after the Wall fell, thus prevented demolition. Studios were built, exhibition spaces, trendy cafés and a cinema again. In the meantime the "Tacheles", as the artists called their building – the word implies 'straight talking' -, has become one of the city of Berlin's attractions.

Probe einer etwas skurrilen Theatergruppe für den sommerlichen Auftritt im »Tacheles«.
Rehearsal by a somewhat absurd theatre group for a summer appearance in the "Tacheles".

Im Innern des einstigen Passage-Kaufhauses und späteren Hauses der Technik an der Friedrichstraße / Ecke Oranienburger Straße, 1928.
Inside the former Passage department store and later Haus der Technik at the Friedrichstrasse / Oranienburger Strasse junction, 1928.

Auf dem weitläufigen Hof des »Tacheles« in Berlin-Mitte mit der Hinterfront
des Kunsthauses.
*In the extensive courtyard of the "Tacheles" in the Mitte district of Berlin with
the rear façade of the Art-Centre.*

Die Weidendammer Brücke, auf der die Friedrichstraße die Spree überquert, bildete Ende des 17. Jahrhunderts den Übergang zwischen der
Dorotheenstadt und der Spandauer Vorstadt. Im 18. Jahrhundert bürger-
te sich nach dem mit Weiden bestandenen Straßendamm der heutige
Name ein, ihr charakteristisches Aussehen mit den reich geschmückten
Geländern und den vier schmiedeeisernen Kandelabern erhielt sie Ende
des 19. Jahrhunderts. Am nördlichen Spreeufer führt der Schiffbauerdamm bis zur Luisenstraße und unterquert hierbei die Eisenbahnbrücke
direkt am Bahnhof Friedrichstraße. Der Bahnhof war bis zum Fall der

Mauer Grenzübergang zwischen Ost- und Westberlin. Hermetisch ab-
geriegelt und bewacht von Grenzpolizisten mit Maschinengewehren
waren bis Ende 1989 die Bahnsteige, von denen aus die Züge Richtung
Westen fuhren. Durch ein extra dafür errichtetes verglastes Kontroll-
gebäude gelangte man wie durch eine Schleuse zu Fernbahn, S- und
U-Bahn. Unter dem Namen »Tränenpalast« ist das Gebäude inzwischen
zu einem beliebten Veranstaltungs- und Ausstellungsort geworden.
Kabarett, Rock, Varieté und avantgardistische Künstler haben hier eine
ganz eigene Aufführungsmöglichkeit gefunden.

Die Weidendammer Brücke; ihr Wahrzeichen sind zwei schmiedeeiserne Adler,
die auf jeder Seite das kunstvoll gearbeitete Geländer aus den Jahren 1895/96
schmücken.
*The Weidendamm Bridge; its distinctive features are two wrought-iron eagles
that adorn each side of the artfully worked railings dating from 1895/96.*

The Weidendamm Bridge, which takes Friedrichstrasse over the Spree,
was the transition from the Dorotheenstadt and the Spandauer Vorstadt
districts in the late 17th century. The present name caught on because
the roadway (Damm) was lined with willows (Weiden), and the bridge
acquired its characteristic appearance with lavishly decorated railings
and four wrought-iron candelabras in the late 19th century. On the north
bank of the Spree the Schiffbauerdamm leads to Luisenstrasse and thus
passes under the railway bridge next to Bahnhof Friedrichstrasse.
Before the Wall fell the station was a border crossing between East
and West Berlin. Until late 1989 the platforms from which trains left for
the West were hermetically sealed and guarded by border police with
machine guns. A custom-built, glazed passport control building led to
the main line trains, S-Bahn and U-Bahn as if through a lock. Now
known as the "Tränenpalast" ("Palace of Tears"), the building has
developed into a popular events and exhibition venue. Cabaret, rock,
variety and avant-garde artists have found the venue suitable for highly
personal performances.

Am Schiffbauerdamm, der Berühmtheit vor allem durch das Berliner Ensemble
erlangte, reihen sich bis zum Bahnhof Restaurants aneinander, hier die bewach-
sene Fassade des »Engelbrecht«.
In the Schiffbauerdamm, famous above all for the Berliner Ensemble, one res-
taurant follows another up to the station. This is the overgrown façade of the
"Engelbrecht".

Im Sommer erweitern die Restaurants am Schiffbauerdamm ihr Terrain auf das
Trottoir direkt am Wasser. Im Hintergrund der Bahnhof Friedrichstraße, inzwischen aufwändig saniert und auch als Einkaufszentrum ein Anziehungspunkt.
In the summer the restaurants in Schiffbauerdamm spread out on to the pave-
ment right by the water. In the background is Bahnhof Friedrichstrasse, now
elaborately refurbished and also attractive as a shopping centre.

59

Nach der Gründung des Kaiserreichs im Jahr 1871 tagte das neu ge-
wählte deutsche Parlament zunächst an mehreren Orten, bis 1894 nach
einer über zehnjährigen Bauzeit das Reichstagsgebäude am Königsplatz
(heute Platz der Republik) eingeweiht wurde. Architekt des Hauses war
Paul Wallot. Am 9. November 1918 rief von einem Fenster des Reichstags der Sozialdemokrat Philipp Scheidemann die deutsche Republik
aus. Während der Weimarer Republik war der Reichstag Ort heftiger
Debatten zwischen den Parteien, bis am 30. Januar 1933 Hitler an die
Macht kam. Der Reichstagsbrand in der Nacht zum 28. Februar, dessen
Ursache nie eindeutig geklärt wurde, markierte den Beginn einer zwölf
Jahre dauernden nationalsozialistischen Gewaltherrschaft. In den letz-
ten Tagen des Zweiten Weltkriegs wurde das Reichstagsgebäude hart
umkämpft; hier hissten am 30. April 1945 Rotarmisten ihre Fahne über
Berlin. Die Wiederherstellung des arg zerstörten Gebäudes als Depen-
dance des Deutschen Bundestages zog sich bis 1972 hin. Nach der
Wiedervereinigung und dem beschlossenen Umzug des Parlaments von
Bonn nach Berlin erfuhr das Gebäude nach Plänen Fosters eine völlige
Umgestaltung, die 1999 endgültig abgeschlossen war.

*After the foundation of the Empire in 1871 the newly elected parlia-
ment met in various places at first, until the Reichstag building in
Königsplatz (now Platz der Republik) was completed in 1894, after being under construction for ten years. The architect was Paul Wallot. The
Social Democrat Philipp Scheidemann proclaimed the German Republic
from a window in the Reichstag on 9 November 1918. The Reichstag
was the scene of heated debates between the parties under the
Weimar Republic, until Hitler came to power on 30 January 1933. The
Reichstag fire on the night of 27 February, whose cause was never fully*

Das Hauptportal des Reichstagsgebäudes mit der Inschrift »Dem Deutschen
Volke« ist Sitz des Deutschen Bundestages.
*The main portal of the Reichstag building, seat of the German parliament,
carries the inscription "Dem Deutschen Volke" – "To the German People".*

Wie schon den historischen Bau krönt eine Kuppel das Reichstagsgebäude; die
moderne gläserne Kuppel entwarf der englische Architekt Sir Norman Foster.
*The Reichstag is topped with a dome, like the historical building; the modern
glass dome was designed by the British architect Sir Norman Foster.*

explained, marked the beginning of twelve years of National Socialist
tyranny. The Reichstag building was hard fought over in the last days of
the Second World War; Red Army soldiers hoisted their flag over Berlin
on 30 April 1945. The restoration of the severely damaged building as
the Berlin seat of the German parliament continued until 1972. After reunification and the decision to move the parliament from Bonn to Berlin
the building was completely redesigned to plans by Foster, and work
was finally completed in 1999.

Den großartigen Blick auf die Stadt von der begehbaren Kuppel über dem
Plenarsaal des Deutschen Bundestages genießen täglich Hunderte Besucher.
Hundreds of visitors a day enjoy the magnificent view of the city from inside
the dome over the German parliament's plenary chamber.

CHANCELLERY

Am 20. Juni 1991 entschieden die Abgeordneten des Deutschen Bundestages, Berlin wieder zur Hauptstadt und zum Regierungssitz des wiedervereinigten Deutschlands zu machen. Als zentraler Ort für die neu zu errichtenden Regierungsbauten wählte man den Spreebogen nördlich des Reichstagsgebäudes, dem künftigen Tagungsort des Parlaments. 1993 gewannen Axel Schultes und Charlotte Frank den städtebaulichen Ideenwettbewerb, in dem das Bundeskanzleramt als ein Teil des »Band des Bundes« vorgesehen war. Dieses architektonische Ensemble verbindet die einzelnen Regierungsbauten und symbolisiert so den politischen Dialog zwischen Regierung, Parlament und Institu-

tionen. 1997 wurde mit den Arbeiten begonnen und 2001 konnte der Bundeskanzler sein neues Domizil in Besitz nehmen. Bis zur Fertigstellung hatte er nach seinem Umzug aus Bonn vorübergehend im ehemaligen Staatsratsgebäude residiert – wo einst Walter Ulbricht und Erich Honecker ihren Amtssitz hatten.

On 20 June 1991 the members of the German parliament voted to make Berlin capital again, and the seat of government for a reunified Germany. The bend in the river Spree north of the Reichstag, the future seat of parliament, was selected as a central location for the new

Eingang zum Hauptgebäude des Bundeskanzleramts, davor die Plastik »Berlin« des baskischen Künstlers Eduardo Chillida.
Entrance to the main building of the Chancellery, with the "Berlin" sculpture by the Basque artist Eduardo Chillada in front of it.

government buildings that were to be erected. Axel Schultes and Charlotte Frank won the urban development competition, which saw the
Chancellery as part of the "Federal Band", in 1993. This architectural
ensemble links the individual government buildings, thus symbolizing
the political dialogue between government, parliament and institutions.
Work started in 1997, and the Chancellor was able to move into his
new domicile in 2001. After moving from Bonn and before it was completed he had lived temporarily in the former East German government
building – where Walter Ulbricht and Erich Honecker used to have their
official seat.

Wartende Gäste unter dem schützenden Sonnensegel vor dem Eingang des
Kanzleramts.
*Guests waiting under the protective awning outside the entrance to the
Chancellery.*

Nächtlicher Blick in den Ehrenhof des Bundeskanzleramts.
Night view into the courtyard of the Federal Chancellery.

Am Spreebogen, wo Hitlers Architekt Albert Speer einst die überdimensionierte Halle des Volkes plante und wo sich noch 1989 an der Grenze zwischen Ost- und Westberlin Brachland ausbreitete, ist seit den neunziger Jahren ein völlig neues Stadtviertel mit beeindruckenden Regierungsbauten entstanden. In gleicher Linie mit dem Bundeskanzleramt, im Verlauf des »Band des Bundes«, wurde nach Plänen des Münchener Architekten Stephan Braunfels ein Komplex mit Abgeordnetenbüros, Sitzungssälen und einer großen Parlamentsbibliothek errichtet: westlich der Spree das Paul-Löbe-Haus – benannt nach dem SPD-Politiker und letzten demokratischen Reichstagspräsidenten der Weimarer Republik – und am Ostufer das Marie-Elisabeth-Lüders-Haus – benannt nach der liberalen Politikerin und langjährigen Bundestagsabgeordneten. Die Gebäude sind durch einen Fußgängertunnel für die Abgeordneten und ihre Mitarbeiter miteinander verbunden. Über die Spree führt eine Fußgängerbrücke, die auch für die Öffentlichkeit zugänglich ist.

Since the 1990s a completely new urban district containing impressive government buildings has sprung up on the Spree Bend, where Hitler's architect Albert Speer once planned his grotesquely large Hall of the People, and which until 1989 was derelict land on the border between East and West Berlin. A complex with members' offices, conference

rooms and a large parliamentary library was built to plans by the Munich architect Stephan Braunfels on the same line as the Chancellery, as part of the "Federal Band": west of the Spree is the Paul-Löbe-Haus – named after the SPD politician and last democratic Reichstag president under the Weimar Republic – and on the east bank the Marie-Elisabeth-Lüders-Haus – named after the liberal politician and long-standing Bundestag member. The buildings are linked by a tunnel for members and their employees. A pedestrian bridge, accessible to the public, leads over the Spree.

Als Bürogebäude für die Bundestagsabgeordneten wurde das Paul-Löbe-Haus errichtet, Ansicht von der Paul-Löbe-Straße.
The Paul-Löbe-Haus was built to provide offices for members of the Bundestag. View from Paul-Löbe-Strasse.

Am Paul-Löbe-Haus in der Otto-von-Bismarck-Allee.
By the Paul-Löbe-Haus in Otto-von-Bismarck-Allee.

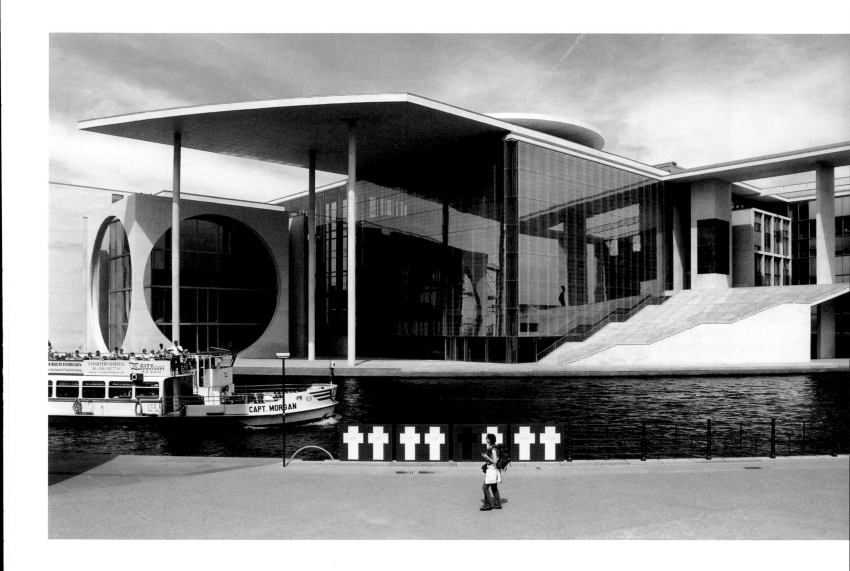

Blick von den Treppen auf der Rückseite des Reichstags über die Spree zum
Marie-Elisabeth-Lüders-Haus. Am Geländer des Reichstagufers Gedenkkreuze
für DDR-Flüchtlinge, die von DDR-Grenzern erschossen wurden.
View from the steps at the back of the Reichstag over the Spree to the Marie-
Elisabeth-Lüders-Haus. On the railings by the Reichstag bank are memorial
crosses for the GDR refugees shot by GDR border guards.

Zur Interbau, der Internationalen Bauausstellung 1957, entstand zwischen Spree und Tiergarten die Kongresshalle nach Plänen des amerikanischen Architekten Hugh A. Stubbins. Die damals Aufsehen erregende Dachkonstruktion stürzte 1980 aufgrund von Materialermüdung und Korrosion überraschend ein, wurde aber zum 750. Jubiläum der Stadt Berlin wieder errichtet. Seit 1989 beherbergt das Gebäude das Haus der Kulturen der Welt und ist seitdem ein gefragter Ort für internationale Ausstellungen und Veranstaltungen.

Gegenüber im Tiergarten treffen sich an Wochenenden vor allem türkische Familien gern zum Picknick. Der Große Tiergarten ist die größte und auch die älteste öffentliche Grünanlage der Stadt. Schon Friedrich II. ließ das Gelände mit den Jagdgehegen von Wenzeslaus von Knobelsdorff zu einem Park mit Goldfischteich, Alleen und Statuen für die Berliner umgestalten. Im 19. Jahrhundert schuf dann Peter Joseph Lenné hier einen großzügigen Landschaftspark, der in vielen Teilen noch erhalten ist.

Die Kongresshalle im Tiergarten, das Haus der Kulturen der Welt. Davor die Plastik »Large Butterfly« des englischen Bildhauers Henry Moore.
The Kongresshalle in the Tiergarten, the House of World Cultures. In front is the English artist Henry Moore's sculpture "Large Butterfly".

The Kongresshalle was built between the Spree and the Tiergarten to plans by the American architect Hugh Stubbins for Interbau, the International Building Exhibition in 1957. The roof construction caused quite a stir at the time it was built; it collapsed surprisingly as a result of material fatigue and corrosion in 1980, but was rebuilt for Berlin's 750th anniversary celebrations. The building has accommodated the House of World Cultures since 1989, and since then it has been in demand as a location for international exhibitions and events. Turkish families in par-

ticular like to meet in the Tiergarten opposite for weekend picnics. The Grosser Tiergarten is the city's largest, and also oldest, green space. These former game reserves were redesigned as long ago as the reign of Frederick II by Wenzeslaus von Knobelsdorff, at the king's behest, to create a park with goldfish pond, avenues and statues for the people of Berlin. Then in the 19th century Peter Joseph Lenné realized an extensive landscaped park which has survived in many areas.

Die Amazone zu Pferde, eine Nachbildung des Originals von Louis Tuaillon aus dem Jahr 1895 im Tiergarten. Nach 1945 herrschten Kälte und Hunger in Berlin, der Tiergarten war abgeholzt, man pflanzte Kartoffeln. Im Hintergrund das sowjetische Ehrenmal und der Reichstag, Fotografie von 1947.
The Amazon on Horseback, a copy of Louis Tuaillon's 1805 original in the Tiergarten. After 1945, Berlin suffered from cold and hunger, the trees in the Tiergarten had been felled and potatoes were planted. In the background is the Soviet War Memorial and the Reichstag, photograph dating from 1947.

Picknick im Tiergarten.
Picnic in the Tiergarten.

Die Siegessäule gehört schon lange zu den bekanntesten Wahrzeichen Berlins. Auf dem Großen Stern steht sie jedoch erst seit dem Jahr 1939, damals wurde sie im Zuge von Hitlers Planungen zur Welthauptstadt »Germania« von ihrem Standort gegenüber dem Reichstag hierher versetzt. Dort, auf dem Königsplatz, war sie bereits 1873 als ein Denkmal eingeweiht worden, das an die Siege Preußens über Dänemark (1864), Österreich (1866) und Frankreich (1870/71) erinnern sollte. Den Sockel der damals 61,5 Meter hohen Säule – entworfen von Johann Heinrich Strack – schmücken Reliefdarstellungen mit Szenen aus diesen drei Kriegen. Gekrönt wird die Säule von der 8,32 Meter hohen Siegesgöttin des Bildhauers Friedrich Drake – von den Berlinern wegen ihres strahlenden Aussehens bald »Goldelse« genannt. Bei ihrer Versetzung erhielt die Säule ein zusätzliches Segment, sodass sie nunmehr 69 Meter hoch ist. Über eine Wendeltreppe in ihrem Inneren gelangt man auf die Aussichtsplattform unter der Viktoria und hat von hier aus einen herrlichen Rundumblick über den Tiergarten und ganz Berlin.

The Siegessäule has long been one of Berlin's best-known landmarks. But it has only stood at the Grosser Stern since 1939, when it was moved there from its site opposite the Reichstag as part of Hitler's plans for his world capital, "Germania". It was dedicated in Königsplatz as early as 1873, intended as a memorial column to Prussia's victories over Denmark (1864), Austria (1866) and France (1870/71). The plinth for the column, which was then 61.5 metres high – designed by Johann Heinrich Strack – is decorated with reliefs of scenes from these three wars. The column is topped by an 8.32 metres high victory goddess by the sculptor Friedrich Drake – soon christened "Goldelse" ("Golden Elsie") by the Berliners because she gleamed so brightly. The column gained an additional segment when it was moved, meaning that it is now 69 metres high. An interior spiral staircase leads to the viewing platform under the victory goddess, from which there is a magnificent panorama of the Tiergarten and the whole of Berlin.

Die Siegessäule auf dem Königsplatz (heute Platz der Republik), dem ursprünglichen Standort, um 1930. Gegenüber das 1894 fertig gestellte Reichstagsgebäude.
The Siegessäule in Königsplatz (now Platz der Republik), its original location. Opposite is the Reichstag building, completed in 1894.

Musiker zu Füßen der Siegessäule.
Musicians under the Siegessäule.

Die vergoldete Viktoria über der Aussichtsplattform der Siegessäule auf
dem Großen Stern.
*The gilded victory goddess above the viewing platform on the Siegessäule at
the Grosser Stern.*

SCHLOSS BELLEVUE

Für den jüngsten Bruder Friedrichs II., den Prinzen August Ferdinand von Preußen, errichtete Baumeister Philipp Daniel Boumann 1785/86 das Schloss Bellevue. Der Prinz hatte bis dahin sein Sommerschloss in Friedrichsfelde, wollte aber etwas näher an der Stadt sein. Das nach barocken Vorbildern, aber schon mit klassizistischen Elementen entstandene Gebäude bildete den architektonischen Endpunkt der barocken Sichtachse vom Octogon (später Leipziger Platz). Nach unterschiedlichen Nutzungen in den folgenden Jahrhunderten wurde es 1955 zum zweiten – Berliner – Amtssitz des Bundespräsidenten bestimmt. Nach der Wiedervereinigung 1993 erklärte Bundespräsident Richard von Weizsäcker Schloss Bellevue zum Hauptsitz des Präsidenten der Bundesrepublik Deutschland. Der Schlossgarten, einst eine der schönsten Parkanlagen vor den Toren Berlins, ist seither aus Sicherheitsgründen für die Öffentlichkeit gesperrt. 2004 wurde mit umfangreichen Restaurierungsmaßnahmen am Schloss begonnen.

Master builder Philipp Daniel Boumann built Schloss Bellevue for the Frederick II's youngest brother, Prince August Ferdinand of Prussia, in 1785/86. The prince's summer palace had been in Friedrichsfelde till then, but he wanted to be nearer town. The building is based on baroque models but already has neo-classical elements. It provides an architectural conclusion to the baroque visual axis running from the Octogon (later Leipziger Platz). After being used in various ways in subsequent centuries it became the German President's second official residence, in Berlin, in 1955. After reunification in 1993, President Richard von Weizsäcker pronounced that Schloss Bellevue was now the German President's first official residence. The Schloss gardens, once one of the most beautiful parks outside the gates of Berlin, has been closed to the public since then for reasons of security. Extensive restoration started in the Schloss in 2004.

Das Bundespräsidialamt am Spreeweg, errichtet nach Plänen der Architekten Martin Gruber und Helmut Kleine-Kraneburg.
The President's Office in Spreeweg, built to plans by architects Martin Gruber and Helmut Kleine-Kraneburg.

Schloss Bellevue am Spreeweg 1 im nördlichen Tiergarten ist der Sitz des
Bundespräsidenten.
*Schloss Bellevue at 1 Spreeweg in the northern Tiergarten is the President's
official seat.*

Die Geschichte des Potsdamer Platzes ist eng mit den jüngsten historischen Entwicklungen verbunden, denn die Grenze zwischen Ost und West verlief genau hier. Nach dem Mauerbau war das gesamte Gelände eine Brache, durchschnitten von den Grenzanlagen. Nichts erinnerte mehr daran, dass der Potsdamer Platz in den zwanziger Jahren einer der belebtesten und verkehrsreichsten Plätze Europas gewesen war, denn am westlichen Ende des Leipziger Platzes, dem Übergang vom alten Zentrum zum Neuen Westen, hatte sich seit dem Ende des 19. Jahrhunderts ein vor allem für seine zahlreichen Vergnügungsstätten bekannter Platz herausgebildet. Im Zweiten Weltkrieg wurde viel zerstört, darunter auch der Potsdamer Bahnhof – bereits 1838 eröffnet – und das Pschorr-Haus. Am 17. Juni 1953, dem Tag des DDR-Volksaufstandes, trafen hier Protestierende auf sowjetische Panzer. Mit dem Mauerfall im November 1989 rückte die Ödnis schlagartig in die Mitte der Metropole zurück. Aus dem verschwundenen Platz wuchs seit Mitte der neunziger Jahre wieder ein neues Stadtquartier empor, das inzwischen längst zum Symbol der pulsierenden Stadt Berlin geworden ist.

The story of Potsdamer Platz is closely linked with recent historical developments, as the border between East and West ran right through it. After the Wall was built the whole area was waste land, bisected by the frontier constructions. There was nothing to remind people that Potsdamer Platz had been one of the liveliest and busiest squares in Europe in the twenties: from the late 19th century it had become a place well known above all for its numerous amusements at the west end of Leipziger Platz, the transition from the old centre to the new west. A great deal was destroyed in the Second World War, including the Potsdam Station – opened as early as 1838 – and the Pschorr Building. On 17 June 1953, the day of the popular uprising in the GDR, protestors were confronted with Soviet tanks here. When the Wall fell in November 1989 this wilderness suddenly shifted back into the centre of the city. From the mid nineties a new urban quarter emerged from the square that had disappeared, and this has now long been a symbol of the vibrant city of Berlin.

Eingang zum unterirdisch angelegten Regionalbahnhof Potsdamer Platz, erbaut nach Plänen des Büros Hilmer & Sattler.
Entrance to Potsdamer Platz underground regional station, built to plans by the Hilmer & Sattler practice.

Wo sich jetzt das Hochhaus von Kollhoff erhebt, stand 1928 der Pschorr-Bierpalast. Links geht die Potsdamer Straße ab (heute Alte Potsdamer Straße).
The Pschorr Beer Palace used to stand on the site of Kollhof's skyscraper. Potsdamer Strasse (now Alte Potsdamer Strasse) goes off on the left.

Das Entree zum Potsdamer Platz von Osten bilden die Hochhäuser beidseitig
der Potsdamer Straße. Links der 101 Meter hohe Klinkerbau von Hans Kollhoff,
der vom gläsernen Turm des Architekten Helmut Jahn nur um zwei Meter
überragt wird.
*The two skyscrapers on either side of Potsdamer Strasse form the gateway
to Potsdamer Platz from the east. On the left is Hans Kollhoff's 101 metre high
brick building; the architect Helmut Jahn's tower is only two metres higher.*

75

Um den Potsdamer Platz nach jahrzehntelanger Vergessenheit im Grenzgebiet zwischen Ost und West wieder zu einem der belebtesten Plätze
Berlins werden zu lassen, lud die Stadt 1991 Architekturbüros aus aller
Welt zum öffentlichen »Ideenwettbewerb Potsdamer/Leipziger Platz«
ein. Auf dem Areal zwischen dem Lenné-Dreieck im Norden, dem Landwehrkanal im Süden, dem Kulturforum im Westen und der Leipziger
Straße im Osten sollte ein neues attraktives Stadtquartier entstehen.
Auf der Grundlage von Plänen der Wettbewerbssieger Hilmar & Sattler
für das gesamte Gebiet entstanden Renzo Pianos DaimlerChrysler-Areal
südlich der Potsdamer Straße und Helmut Jahns Sony-Areal nördlich
davon. In nur wenigen Jahren wuchsen hier auf der »größten Baustelle
Europas« Bürogebäude, eine Shopping Mall, Kinozentren, Restaurants
und Cafés, ein Hotel und ein Musical-Theater in die Höhe. Im Oktober
1994 hatte die Grundsteinlegung für das DaimlerChrysler-Areal stattgefunden und schon am 2. Oktober 1998 konnte es mit einer großen Feier
eingeweiht werden.

*In 1991, Berlin invited architects from all over the world to take part in
a public "Competition for Potsdamer/Leipziger Platz", in order to make
Potsdamer Platz one of Berlin's liveliest squares again, after decades of
lying forgotten in the border area between East and West. A new and
attractive urban quarter was to come into being on the site bounded to
the north by the Lenné Triangle, the Landwehr canal to the south, the
Kulturforum to the west and Leipziger Strasse to the east. Renzo Piano's
DaimlerChrysler site was built south of Potsdamer Strasse and Helmut
Jahn's Sony site to the north of it, on the basis of plans by competition
winners Hilmer & Sattler. In a very few years, a shopping mall, cinema
centres, restaurants and cafés, a hotel and a musical theatre sprang up
on "Europe's largest building site". The foundation stone on the DaimlerChrysler plot was laid in October 1994 and it was opened amidst
great celebrations as early as 2 October 1998.*

Die Skulptur »Galileo« des Künstlers Mark di Suvero inmitten der Wasserfläche
zwischen Marlene-Dietrich-Platz und Reichpietschufer am Landwehrkanal.
*The "Galileo" sculpture by the artist Mark di Suvero in the middle of the stretch
of water between Marlene-Dietrich-Platz and the Reichpietschufer on the Landwehr canal.*

Blick vom Marlene-Dietrich-Platz in Richtung Südosten, links das IMAX-Kino
und rechts die debis-Zentrale. Die Gebäude entstanden nach Entwürfen des
italienischen Architekten Renzo Piano.
*View from Marlene-Dietrich-Platz looking south-east. On the left is the IMAX
cinema and on the right the debis headquarters. The buildings were designed
by the Italian architect Renzo Piano.*

77

Nähert man sich vom Tiergarten dem Potsdamer Platz, erscheint dieser wie eine eigene Stadt vor den Toren Berlins. Mitte des 18. Jahrhunderts, als sich hier die ersten Hugenotten ansiedelten, lag das Gelände auch noch westlich der Zollmauer. Da die Berliner auf ihren Ausflügen in den nahe gelegenen Tiergarten hier entlangpromenierten, gab es bald etliche Stände, an denen es Kleinigkeiten zu essen und zu trinken gab, und aus denen bald die ersten Cafés und Restaurants entstanden. Berühmt war vor allem das Café Josty, das noch bis ins 20. Jahrhundert hinein existierte. Den Namen erhielt der Platz 1831 nach dem Potsdamer Tor, das von Schinkel 1823/24 dort errichtet worden war. Zu einem kräftigen Aufschwung kam es nach der Eröffnung des Potsdamer Bahnhofs, 1838 fuhr von hier die erste Berliner Eisenbahn – zunächst nach Zehlendorf, dann bis Potsdam und später Richtung Magdeburg. Es entstanden Hotels und zahlreiche Vergnügungsstätten, die wie das »Haus Vaterland« weit über die Grenzen Berlins hinaus bekannt waren.

When approached from the east via the Tiergarten, Potsdamer Platz seems like a city in its own right outside the gates of Berlin. In the mid 18th century, when the first Huguenots settled here, the site was still west of the customs wall. The people of Berlin used to promenade along here on their excursions to the Tiergarten, so stalls quickly appeared selling snacks and drinks, and these became the first cafés and restaurants. The Café Josty, which survived into the 20th century, was the most famous. The square was named in 1831 from the Potsdam Gate, which Schinkel built there in 1823/24. The area was powerfully boosted by the opening of the Potsdam Station, from which the first Berlin railway ran – first to Zehlendorf, then to Potsdam and later in the direction of Magdeburg. Hotels and various leisure facilities established themselves here, some of them, like "Haus Vaterland", being known well beyond the confines of Berlin.

Nächtlicher Blick vom Kulturforum im Westen auf den Potsdamer Platz, links das Sony-Areal, rechts das DaimlerChrysler-Areal.
Night view from the Kulturforum to the west of Potsdamer Platz. The Sony site is on the left and the DaimlerChrysler buildings are on the right.

Das Forum des von Helmut Jahn entworfenen SonyCenter wird von einer ungewöhnlichen Dachkonstruktion überspannt, einem Wetterschutz aus Stahl, Glas und Glasfasergewebe.
The Forum in Helmut Jahn's SonyCenter is spanned by an unusual roof structure in steel, glass and fibre-glass cloth, affording protection from the weather.

PHILHARMONIE

Die 1960–63 errichtete Philharmonie und der benachbarte Kammermusiksaal sind Stammspielorte der Berliner Philharmoniker. Das alte Gebäude der Philharmonie in der Bernburger Straße war 1944 bei einem Luftangriff zerstört worden. Nach dem Krieg hatte das Orchester zunächst im Steglitzer Titania-Palast gespielt und später im Konzertsaal der Hochschule für Musik in Charlottenburg. Wie die jenseits der Potsdamer Straße gelegene Staatsbibliothek wurden die Konzertgebäude nach Plänen Hans Scharouns errichtet. Auf die Idee Scharouns geht auch die Errichtung des Kulturforums zurück, in das alle drei Häuser einbezogen sind. Zu Zeiten der Teilung der Stadt sollte hier ein neues kulturelles Zentrum entstehen – als Ersatz für all die Gebäude, die im Zweiten Weltkrieg zerstört worden waren sowie für jene, die im Ostteil der Stadt lagen und somit für Westberliner unzugänglich. Inzwischen gehören zum Kulturforum verschiedene Museen, darunter das Musikinstrumentenmuseum und die Neue Nationalgalerie.

The Philharmonie and adjacent Kammermusiksaal are the Berlin Philharmonic's permanent homes for concerts and chamber music. The old Philharmonie building in Bernburger Strasse was destroyed in an air raid in 1944. After the war the orchestra first played in the Titania-Palast in Steglitz, and later in the concert hall in the Music College in Charlottenburg. Like the Staatsbibliothek on the other side of Potsdamer Strasse, the concert buildings were built to plans by Hans Scharoun. Scharoun was also responsible for the idea of building the Kulturforum, which included all three institutions. A new cultural centre was intended to emerge here while the city was divided – as a substitute for all the buildings that had been destroyed in the Second World War, and for those that were in the eastern part of the city, and thus inaccessible to West Berliners. The Kulturforum now contains varions museums, f. e. the Museum of Musical Instruments and the Neue Nationalgalerie .

Ein vorübergehend am Leipziger Platz verankerter Sat.1-Ballon über den Dächern des Kammermusiksaals und des SonyCenter.
A Sat.1 balloon, temporarily anchored in Leipziger Platz, above the roofs of the Kammermusiksaal and the SonyCenter.

Eingang zur Philharmonie am Kemperplatz, errichtet 1960–63.
Entrance to the Philharmonie in Kemperplatz, built 1960–63.

Das Kulturforum, aufgenommen von der Aussichtsplattform des Kollhoff-Gebäudes am Potsdamer Platz: In der Bildmitte links die von Mies van der Rohe errichtete Neue Nationalgalerie, rechts davon schließen sich die St.-Matthäus-Kirche und die Gemäldegalerie an. Am rechten Bildrand der Kammermusiksaal und die Philharmonie.

The Kulturforum taken from the observation platform atop the Kollhoff building on Potsdamer Platz. The photograph's left, at middle, is Mies van der Rohe's Neue Nationalgalerie, to the right of which are the St.-Matthäus-Kirche (St Mathew's Church) and the Gemäldegalerie. The Kammermusiksaal (Chamber Concert Hall) and the Philharmonie are at the far right.

Die St.-Matthäus-Kirche ist das einzige Gebäude, das von der histori-schen Bebauung im Bereich des Kulturforums übrig geblieben ist. Der 1844–46 nach Plänen Friedrich August Stülers errichtete Ziegelbau stand einstmals inmitten des so genannten Geheimratsviertels, einer geschlossenen Wohnhausbebauung zwischen Landwehrkanal und Tier-garten. Schon 1938 erfolgte der Abriss zahlreicher Gebäude für das Haus des Fremdenverkehrs, das den von Albert Speer geplanten Runden Platz der Nord-Süd-Achse der Welthauptstadt »Germania« säumen sollte. Es wurde wie das gesamte Viertel im Zweiten Weltkrieg zerstört und Ende der fünfziger, Anfang der sechziger Jahre abgerissen, lediglich die Kirche baute man wieder auf. Die Neue Nationalgalerie, ein Meis-terwerk des Architekten Mies van der Rohe, entstand nach Scharouns Philharmonic 1965 als zweites Gebäude am Kulturforum. Die Potsdamer Straße erhielt im Zuge der neuen Planungen einen anderen Verlauf; auf dem Terrain der alten steht heute die Staatsbibliothek.

The St.-Matthäus-Kirche is the only historical building to have survived in the Kulturforum area. This brick structure, built to plans by Friedrich August Stüler in 1844–46, stood in the middle of the so-called Geheim-ratsviertel, a unified residential development between the Landwehr canal and the Tiergarten. Numerous buildings were pulled down as early as 1938 to make way for the Haus des Fremdenverkehrs, which was intended to border Albert Speer's planned Runder Platz on the north-south axis of the world capital "Germania". This building was badly damaged in the Second World War, as was the whole district, and pulled down in the late fifties, early sixties. Only the church was rebuilt. The Neue Nationalgalerie, a masterpiece by the architect Mies van der Rohe, was the second building to go up in the Kulturforum, after Scharoun's Philharmonie. The line of Potsdamer Strasse was changed in the course of the new developments; the Staatsbibliothek (national library) now stands on the land occupied by the old street.

Blick auf die St.-Matthäus-Kirche am Kulturforum, rechts die Rückseite der Neuen Nationalgalerie.
View of the St.-Matthäus-Kirche (St Mathew's Church) by the Kulturforum, on the right is the back of the Neue Nationalgalerie.

Luftaufnahme von 1945; links oben die Ruine der St.-Matthäus-Kirche, in der Mitte der Komplex vom Haus des Fremdenverkehrs an der Potsdamer Straße, vorn die Potsdamer Brücke über den Landwehrkanal.
Aerial photograph taken in 1945, on the left are the ruins of the St.-Matthäus-Kirche (St Mathew's Church), in the middle is the Haus des Fremdenverkehrs complex (tourism) in Potsdamer Strasse.

Eingangsbereich des Kulturforums, von hier aus gelangt man zu dem Kunstge-werbemuseum, dem Kupferstichkabinett, der Kunstbibliothek und zur Gemälde-galerie.
Entrance area for the Kulturforum, leading to the Kunstgewerbemusem (Arts and Crafts Museum), the Kupferstichkabinett (Collection of Drawings and Prints) and the Gemäldegalerie (Picture Gallery).

Eine der ältesten Einrichtungen der *Stiftung Preußischer Kulturbesitz – Staatliche Museen zu Berlin* ist die Gemäldegalerie. Schon 1830 wurde sie in dem klassizistischen Schinkel-Bau am Lustgarten eröffnet. Dieser erste Museumsbau in Berlin, heute Altes Museum, war auch das erste Gebäude der Museumsinsel. Als es für die ständig gewachsene Sammlung zu klein wurde, erhielt die Gemäldegalerie 1904 mit dem Kaiser-Friedrich-Museum (seit 1956 Bode-Museum) ein neues Domizil an der nördlichen Spitze der Museumsinsel. Während des Zweiten Weltkriegs mussten die Kunstschätze ausgelagert werden, einige sind verschollen oder zerstört. Nach der Spaltung der Stadt in Ost- und Westberlin gab es fortan neben dem Bode-Museum in Ostberlin den Westberliner Standort in Dahlem. Seit 1992 existiert wieder eine einheitliche Leitung, und 1998 konnten alle Gemälde in einem der Bedeutung der Sammlung angemessenen Neubau am Kulturforum wieder zusammengeführt werden. Der Entwurf für das Gebäude, dessen Kuppel über die Dächer des Forums hinausragt, stammt von den Architekten Hilmer und Sattler.

In der Gemäldegalerie; begutachtet wird *Der Jungbrunnen*, 1546 von Lucas Cranach d. Ä. gemalt.
In the Gemäldegalerie, the Jungbrunnen *(Fountain of Youth), painted in 1546 by Lucas Cranach the Elder, is being examined carefully.*

The Gemäldegalerie (Picture Gallery) is one of the oldest institutions of the Stiftung Preussischer Kulturbesitz – Staatliche Museen zu Berlin. It first opened in Schinkel's neo-classical building by the Lustgarten in 1830. This, now the Altes Museum, was the first museum building in Berlin, and also the first building on the Museum Island. When it became too small for the constantly growing collection of paintings, the Gemäldegalerie acquired a new home at the northern tip of the Museum Island in the Kaiser-Friedrich-Museum (Bode-Museum from 1956) in 1904. The art treasures had to be moved out during the Second World War, and some are since missing or were destroyed. After the city was divided into East and West Berlin, there was a West Berlin site in Dahlem, as well as the Bode-Museum in East Berlin. The museum has been a single organization again since 1992, and all the paintings were reunited in a new building in the Kulturforum commensurate with the importance of the collection. This building, with its dome towering over the roofs of the Forum, was designed by the architects Hilmer & Sattler.

In der Gemäldegalerie, unbeachtet: *Venus und Amor als Honigdieb*, nach 1537 von Lucas Cranach d. Ä. gemalt.
Venus und Amor als Honigdieb (Venus with Cupid as Honey Thief), painted after 1537 by Lucas Cranach the Elder, is being ignored.

Pause vor Dirk van Baburens *Fußwaschung Christi.*
Pause at Dirk van Baburen's Fusswaschung Christi
(Christ Washing the Apostles' Feet).

Das Flugzeug über der Fassade des Deutschen Technikmuseums Berlin erinnert an die Luftbrücke der Westalliierten 1948/49.
The plane above the façade of the Deutsches Technikmuseum Berlin (technology) commemorates the Western Allies' airlift in 1948/49.

Das Deutsche Technikmuseum Berlin, mit dessen Einrichtung 1982 an
der Trebbiner Straße in Kreuzberg begonnen wurde, steht an einem
besonderen historischen Ort. Dort, wo heute die Fußgängerbrücke den
Landwehrkanal überquert, fuhren einst die Fernzüge vom Anhalter
Bahnhof in Richtung Süden, und neben dem Gebäude des Museums er-
streckten sich der Anhalter Güterbahnhof und ein Bahnbetriebsgelände.
Als nach der Teilung der Stadt hier keine Züge mehr ankamen, da sie
von der DDR-Verwaltung der Deutschen Reichsbahn umgeleitet wurden,
erfolgte die Stilllegung. Ein großer Teil des Territoriums mit Hallen und
Ringlokschuppen gehört inzwischen zum Museum und ist nach und nach
für den Ausstellungsbereich und den Museumspark erschlossen wor-
den. Im April 2003 konnte der Neubau eröffnet werden. Über seiner
Glasfront ist eine »Skytrain« aufgehängt – solchen Maschinen, die den
Westteil der Stadt während der sowjetischen Blockade 1948/49 mit
allen lebensnotwendigen Gütern versorgten, gaben die Berliner den
Namen »Rosinenbomber«. Der Neubau des Museums beherbergt die
Schiffbau- und seit April 2005 auch die Luftfahrtausstellung.

*The Deutsches Technikmuseum Berlin, first established in 1982 in
Trebbiner Strasse in Kreuzberg, stands on a particularly historical site.
Main-line trains from the Anhalt Station used to run south at the point
where the pedestrian bridge now crosses the Landwehr canal, and the
Anhalt goods station and a railway service plant were sited beside the
museum building. When trains no longer ran here after the city was
divided, as they had been diverted by the GDR administrators of the
Deutsche Reichsbahn, the facilities were closed down. A large part of
the territory with halls and circular engine sheds now belongs to the
museum, and has gradually been developed as an exhibition area and
museum park. The new building was ready to reopen in April 2003.
A "Skytrain" is suspended above its glass façade – the Berliners nick-
named these planes "Rosinenbomber" – raisin bombers: they supplied
the city with all essential commodities during the Soviet blockade in
1948/49. The new building houses the ship-building exhibitions, and,
since April 2005, the aviation exhibitions.*

Die U-Bahnline 1 und die historische Fußgängerbrücke überqueren vor dem
Technikmuseum den Landwehrkanal.
*The U-Bahn Line 1 and the historical pedestrian bridge cross the Landwehr
canal in front of the Technikmuseum.*

TEMPODROM

Im Jahr 1980 konnte sich eine junge Westberlinerin dank einer Erbschaft einen Lebenstraum erfüllen: Sie kaufte ein großes Zelt, in dem 3000 Leute Platz fanden, und gründete zusammen mit Freunden das Tempodrom, einen eigenen Veranstaltungsort für Konzerte, Theater, Tanzveranstaltungen, Partys, Festivals. Standort war die Brache am Potsdamer Platz, direkt an der Mauer. Und es funktionierte. Schon in den ersten Jahren wurde das Tempodrom bei den Berlinern populär. Hier gab es Volks- und Tanzmusik fremder Kulturen, Kabarett, klassische Konzerte, politische Diskussionen und internationale Rock- und Pop-Konzerte. Nach vier Jahren zog das Tempodrom neben die Kongresshalle (heute Haus der Kulturen der Welt) in den Tiergarten um, wo es zu einer festen Berliner Kulturinstitution avancierte. Nach dem Mauerfall, als die Planungen für den Bau des Kanzleramtes in dieser Gegend begannen, stand erneut ein Umzug an. Als neuen Standort bot das Bezirksamt Kreuzberg das Gelände des ehemaligen Anhalter Bahnhofs an. Nun entschloss man sich mit Unterstützung des Senats, ein festes Haus zu bauen. Das nach Plänen von Gerkan, Marg & Partner errichtete Gebäude wurde am 1. Dezember 2001 eröffnet.

In 1980 a young West Berlin woman was able to make one of her dreams come true, thanks to a legacy: she bought a large tent that could accommodate 3000 people and founded the Tempodrom with some of her friends, a separate events venue for concerts, theatre, dances, parties and festivals. It was sited on derelict land in Potsdamer Platz, right by the Wall. And it worked. The Tempodrom was popular with Berliners from the outset. Here they could come to see folk and dance music from other cultures, cabaret, classical concerts, political discussions and international rock and pop concerts. After four years the Tempodrom moved into the Tiergarten near the Kongresshalle (now the House of World Cultures), where it went on to become an established Berlin cultural institution. It had to contend with another move after the Wall fell and plans to build the Chancellery in this area got under way. The district of Kreuzberg offered the site of the former Anhalter Station as a new location. And now a decision was taken, supported by the Senate, to opt for a permanent building. This was built to plans by von Gerkan, Marg & Partner, and opened on 1 December 2001.

Blick auf den im Zweiten Weltkrieg stark zerstörten Anhalter Bahnhof, 1945.
Den Bahnhof gibt es längst nicht mehr, dort wo die Gleise aus der Halle hinausführen, steht heute das Tempodrom.
View of the Anhalter Station, which was badly damaged in the Second World War, in 1945. The station has not existed for a long time, and the Tempodrom now stands where the lines used to run out of the hall.

Abendliche Stimmung vor dem Tempodrom in Kreuzberg.
Evening atmosphere outside the Tempodrom in Kreuzberg.

Schon vor der Eröffnung der Dauerausstellung »Zwei Jahrtausende Deutsch-Jüdische Geschichte« am 9. September 2001 war das neue Gebäude des Jüdischen Museums Berlin ein Anziehungspunkt für Besucher. Tausende kamen, um sich die eigenwillige, verstörende Architektur des amerikanischen Architekten Daniel Libeskind anzusehen. In dem gezackten Grundriss des Hauses mit der zinkverkleideten Fassade sieht der Architekt einen geborstenen Davidstern. Leerräume aus nacktem Beton durchziehen den gesamten Bau in seiner Mitte. Sie symbolisieren den Verlust, der durch die Vernichtung der Juden durch die National-

sozialisten in Europa entstanden ist. Im Untergeschoss kreuzen sich drei Achsen: Die erste führt zur lichten Haupttreppe, die in die hellen Ausstellungsgeschosse nach oben führt, die zweite, ein immer niedriger werdender Gang mit schrägen Wänden und unebenem Boden, führt nach draußen in den Garten des Exils, die dritte ist eine Sackgasse, die im Holocaust-Turm endet. In den Neubau gelangt man über einen unterirdischen Gang vom barocken Eingangsgebäude aus. In dem 1735 erbauten Kollegienhaus befand sich einst das preußische Kammergericht und später das Berlin-Museum.

Installation »Shalechet« (»Gefallenes Laub«) des israelischen Künstlers Menashe Kadishman in einem der Leerräume des Gedenkens (Memory Void) im Libeskind-Bau.
"Shalechet" ("Fallen Leaves") installation by the Israeli artist Menashe Kadishman in one of the Memory Void rooms in Libeskind's building.

Fenster-Einschnitte im Raum der Dauerausstellung des Jüdischen Museums.
Window slits in the Jewish Museum's permanent exhibition gallery.

The Jewish Museum's new building in Berlin attracted visitors even before the permanent exhibition "Two Thousand Years of German-Jewish History" opened on 9 September 2001. Thousands came to look at the American architect Daniel Libeskind's highly individual, distressing architecture. The architect sees the jagged ground plan of the building with its zinc-clad façade as a Star of David that has exploded. Empty spaces in exposed concrete run through the whole of the middle of the building. They symbolize the loss sustained as a result of the National Socialists' annihilation of the Jews in Europe. Three axes cross on the basement floor: the first leads to the bright main steps leading up to the well-lit exhibition floors, the second is a corridor that constantly becomes lower, with slanting walls and an uneven floor, leads out into the Garden of Exile, and the third is a cul-de-sac ending in the Holocaust Tower. Access to the new building is through an underground corridor from the baroque entrance building. This Kollegienhaus, built in 1953, used to house the Prussian Court of Appeal, then later the Berlin-Museum.

Der Garten des Exils und der Emigration am Jüdischen Museum Berlin in der Kreuzberger Lindenstraße.
The Garden of Exile and Emigration at the Jewish Museum Berlin in Lindenstrasse, Kreuzberg.

Das Jüdische Museum in Kreuzberg mit seiner eigenwilligen Architektur von
Daniel Libeskind; links der dazugehörige Holocaust-Turm, rechts davon der
Garten des Exils mit seinen 49 Betonstelen.
*The Jewish Museum in Kreuzberg, with its distinctive architecture by Daniel
Libeskind; the building's Holocaust Tower rises at the far left; the Garden of Exil,
which consists 49 concrete steles, lies directly to its right.*

Nach der Errichtung der Sperrmauer am 13. August 1961 existierten zwischen West- und Ostberlin nur noch acht Grenzübergänge: an der Bornholmer Straße, in der Chausseestraße, in der Invalidenstraße, der Heinrich-Heine-Straße, auf der Oberbaumbrücke für Fußgänger aus Westberlin und an der Sonnenallee. Nur an der Bornholmer Straße zwischen Wedding und Prenzlauer Berg durften Westberliner und Bundesbürger den Übergang gemeinsam benutzen, ansonsten gab es hier eine strenge Trennung. Eine Ausnahme bildete der Bahnhof Friedrichstraße, er war für alle zugänglich – auch für Ausländer, die zu Fuß oder mit dem Auto sonst nur auf der Friedrichstraße nach Ostberlin einreisen konnten. Der Checkpoint Charlie stellte für die DDR-Grenzbehörden einen besonders neuralgischen Punkt dar, da ihnen die Kontrolle ausländischer Diplomaten und Angehöriger der Westalliierten nicht erlaubt war. So bestand für sie immer der Verdacht, dass im Diplomatengepäck etliche verbotene Gegenstände, Schriften, Medien etc. die Seiten wechselten.

After the border Wall was built on 13 August 1961 there were only eight crossing-points between West and East Berlin: at Bornholmer Strasse, Chausseestrasse, Invalidenstrasse, Heinrich-Heine-Strasse, at the Oberbaumbrücke for pedestrians from West Berlin and in Sonnenallee. Only in Bornholmer Strasse, between Wedding and Prenzlauer Berg, were West Berliners and citizens of West Germany allowed

to cross together, otherwise there was strict separation. One exception was Bahnhof Friedrichstrasse, which was available to all – even foreigners, who could otherwise only enter Berlin on foot or by car at Checkpoint Charlie, which was also in Friedrichstrasse. Checkpoint Charlie was a particularly touchy spot for the GDR border authorities, as they were not allowed to check foreign diplomats or relatives of the Western allies. So they always suspected that various forbidden objects, writings, media etc. were changing hands.

Checkpoint Charlie, 26. Oktober 1961. Am 25. Oktober 1961 ließ der amerikanische Stadtkommandant Panzer am Checkpoint Charlie auffahren, nachdem Ostberliner Grenzer einigen amerikanischen Zivilbeamten die Einreise nach Ostberlin verweigert hatten. Daraufhin gingen am 27. Oktober auf der anderen Seite sowjetische Panzer in Stellung.
Checkpoint Charlie, 26 October 1961. On 25 October 1961 the American Town Commandant ordered tanks to Checkpoint Charlie after East Berlin border officials had refused to let American civilians enter East Berlin. Soviet tanks took up positions on the other side on 27 October as a result.

Überreste der einst 155 Kilometer langen Mauer, die Westberlin umschloss.
Remains of the Wall, once 155 kilometres long, that used to enclose West Berlin.

Das Wachhäuschen in der Friedrichstraße, Ecke Zimmerstraße erinnert an den
Checkpoint Charlie, einen der bekanntesten Grenzübergänge zwischen Ost und
West. In unmittelbarer Nähe befindet sich das Mauermuseum.
*The little guard-house at the junction of Friedrichstrasse and Zimmerstrasse is a
reminder of Checkpoint Charlie, one of the best-known East-West border-cros-
sing points. The Mauermuseum (Berlin Wall museum) is immediately adjacent.*

97

WALL MEMORIAL CENTRE

Am 13. August 1961, in der Nacht von Samstag auf Sonntag, riegelten Militäreinheiten der DDR Westberlin ab. Der S-Bahnverkehr wurde unterbrochen, mit Maschinengewehren bewaffnete Grenzpolizisten, Volkspolizisten und Betriebskampfgruppen sperrten die Grenze, rissen die Straßen auf, legten Stacheldrahtrollen aus. In den Monaten und Jahren davor hatten Hunderttausende DDR-Bürger ihre Heimat verlassen und waren zumeist über Westberlin in die Bundesrepublik geflüchtet. Auch wenn der damalige Partei- und Regierungschef Walter Ulbricht die Mauer als »antifaschistischen Schutzwall« bezeichnete, beabsichtigte die DDR mit der Schließung der Grenze nach Westberlin vor allem, den für ihre Wirtschaft katastrophalen Weggang von Fachkräften zu stoppen. Am 15. August wurde mit dem Bau der Mauer begonnen, deren Anlage im Lauf ihres Bestehens immer »perfekter«; viele, die über die Mauer fliehen wollten, fanden hier den Tod. Am 9. November 1989, nach mehr als 28 Jahren, öffneten sich die innerdeutschen Grenzen und binnen weniger Monate war auch die einst undurchdringliche Mauer nur noch Geschichte.

On 13 August 1961, as Saturday passed to Sunday, GDR military units cut West Berlin off. S-Bahn travel was interrupted and border guards with machine guns, People's Police and operational brigades sealed the border, tore up the streets and put down rolls of barbed wire. Hundreds of thousands of GDR citizens had left their homes in the previous months and years and fled to West Germany, usually via West Berlin. Even though the then party leader and head of government Walter Ulbricht called the Wall an "anti-Fascist protective wall", the GDR's main intention in closing the border was to stop the outflow of experts in all fields that was so catastrophic for their economy. Work on constructing the Wall itself started on 15 August, and it became more and more "perfect" the longer it lasted. Many people who tried to flee over the Wall lost their lives here. On 9 November 1989, after over 28 years, the internal German borders were reopened and the once impenetrable Wall was relegated to history within a very few months.

Touristen in der Mauergedenkstätte, die einen Eindruck von der gesamten Grenzanlage vermittelt.
Tourists in the Wall memorial centre, which conveys an impression of the border fortifications as a whole.

Blick auf die Grenzanlagen am Brandenburger Tor, links oben am Bildrand die Säulen des Reichstagsgebäudes, um 1980.
View of the border structures at the Brandenburg Gate, on the top left-hand edge of the picture are the columns of the Reichstag building, c. 1980.

Das Dokumentationszentrum Berliner Mauer in der Bernauer Straße ist eine der wenigen Gedenkstätten mit Überresten des unmenschlichen Bauwerks.
The Berlin Wall documentation centre in Bernauer Strasse is one of the few memorials holding remains of this inhuman construction.

Der Prenzlauer Berg galt schon zu DDR-Zeiten als ein besonderer Bezirk. In den recht preiswerten Altbauten lebten Künstler, Schriftsteller, Studenten, und hier traf sich in den achtziger Jahren die oppositionelle Bürgerbewegung. Nach der Wende kam die alternative Szene aus den westlichen Bezirken dazu, neue Kulturzentren wie die KulturBrauerei und der Pfefferberg entstanden. In Räumen der KulturBrauerei – dort war 1967 das letzte Mal Schultheiss-Bier gebraut worden – hatte es schon seit 1970 den Franz-Klub gegeben, der jedoch 1997 Konkurs anmelden musste. 2000 begann eine umfangreiche Sanierung der gesamten Fabrikanlage, es entstanden Büros, ein Supermarkt, Kinos und zahlreiche Räume für Klubs und Kultur. Auch die Quartiere rundherum erfuhren eine Umgestaltung. Heruntergekommene Wohnungen erhielten mehr Komfort, neue Geschäfte und Restaurants öffneten rund um den Kollwitzplatz. Aus dem Prenzlauer Berg wurde ein Quartier, von dem sich vor allem junge Leute und Familien angezogen fühlen. Inzwischen ist der Bezirk der kinderreichste Berlins.

Even in the GDR days Prenzlauer Berg was considered to be a distinctive district. Artists, writers and students lived in the very reasonably priced old buildings, and the citizens' opposition movement met here in the eighties. After the Wall fell the alternative scene from the western districts joined in, and new culture centres like the KulturBrauerei and the Pfefferberg came into being. The Franz-Klub had existed in the KulturBrauerei's premises since 1970 – Schultheiss beer was brewed there for the last time in 1967 – but it had to declare itself bankrupt in 1997. An extensive refurbishment of the whole factory complex started in 2000, producing offices, a supermarket, cinemas and numerous spaces for clubs and culture. The surrounding quarters were redesigned as well. Dilapidated dwellings were made more comfortable, and new shops and restaurants opened around Kollwitzplatz. Prenzlauer Berg became an area that attracts young people and families above all. The district now has more children than any other in Berlin.

Musikveranstaltung im Biergarten des »Pfefferbergs« an der Schönhauser Allee, gegenüber vom Senefelderplatz. Auch hier befand sich früher eine Brauerei.
Music event in the beer garden of the "Pfefferberg" in Schönhauser Allee, opposite Senefelderplatz. There used to be a brewery here too as well.

Auf einem der Höfe in der KulturBrauerei zwischen Schönhauser Allee, Sredzki- und Knaackstraße. Neben Restaurants und Cafés gibt es hier Klubs, Kinos und Theatersäle.
In one of the yards in the KulturBrauerei between Schönhauser Allee, Sredzki-strasse and Knaackstrasse. There are clubs, theatres and cinemas here as well as cafés and restaurants.

Der Kollwitzplatz mit seinen vielen Restaurants, Cafés und kleinen Geschäften
ist fast schon zu einem Symbol für die neue Lebendigkeit in Prenzlauer Berg
geworden.
*Kollwitzplatz with its many restaurants, cafés and little shops has already come
to symbolize Prenzlauer Berg's new vigour.*

Schon im Mittelalter führte hier eine Handelsstraße nach Frankfurt/ Oder, und im 20. Jahrhundert entwickelte sich die Frankfurter Allee zu einer der wichtigsten Magistralen Berlins. In den letzten Tagen des Zweiten Weltkriegs wurde ein Großteil der bereits durch Bomben beschädigten Häuser während heftiger Straßenkämpfe völlig zerstört. Zu Beginn der fünfziger Jahre begann die DDR-Regierung mit dem Wiederaufbau der Stalinallee, wie die Straße nun hieß. Wohnpaläste für die Arbeiter sollten entstehen, architektonisch orientiert am »Zucker-bäckerstil« sowjetischer Bauten der Stalinzeit. Unter der Leitung des Architekten Hermann Henselmann entwarfen mehrere Architektenkol-lektive für den Abschnitt zwischen Proskauer Straße und Strausberger Platz großzügige, komfortabel ausgestattete Wohnbauten der »ersten sozialistischen Straße Deutschlands«. – Doch ausgerechnet unter den Bauarbeitern der Stalinallee begann im Juni 1953 der Streik, der sich zum Volksaufstand des 17. Juni gegen die SED-Regierung entwickelte und mithilfe sowjetischer Panzer niedergeschlagen wurde. Die Stalin-allee heißt seit 1961 wieder Frankfurter Allee und Karl-Marx-Allee (vom Frankfurter Tor bis zum Alexanderplatz).

A trade road led from here to Frankfurt an der Oder even in the Middle Ages, and Frankfurter Allee became one of Berlin's most important main thoroughfares in the 20th century. The majority of the buildings, already badly damaged by bombs, were completely destroyed by violent street fighting in the last days of the Second World War. The GDR government started to rebuild Stalinallee, as the street was now called, in the early 1950s. The aim was to produce palatial accommodation for the work-ers, modelled architecturally on the "wedding-cake style" of Soviet buildings in the Stalin era. Several architects' collectives, under the direction of the architect Hermann Henselmann, designed spacious, comfortably furnished dwellings for the section between Proskauer Strasse and Strausberger Platz in "Germany's first socialist street". – But it was among the Stalinallee workers of all people that the strike broke out in June 1953 that led to the popular uprising against the Communist Government on 17 June, put down with the aid of Soviet tanks. Stalinallee was renamed Frankfurter Allee and Karl-Marx-Allee (from the Frankfurter Tor to Alexanderplatz) in 1961.

Am Strausberger Platz enden die so genannten Stalin-Bauten aus den fünfziger Jahren an der Karl-Marx-Allee; die Plattenbauten hinter den beiden Turmhäu-sern entstanden in den sechziger Jahren.
The so-called Stalinist buildings dating from the 1950s in Karl-Marx-Allee end at Strausberger Platz; the slab-construction blocks behind the two high-rise buildings date from the 1960s.

Demonstranten auf der Stalinallee am 17. Juni 1953, rechts ein bereits fertig gestellter Block der »sozialistischen Straße«.
Demonstrators in Stalinallee on 17 June 1953, on the right is a section of the "socialist street" that has already been completed.

Die Wohntürme am Frankfurter Tor markieren den Anfang der Karl-Marx-Allee,
Blick von Osten zum Strausberger Platz.
The high-rise blocks at the Frankfurter Tor mark the beginning of Karl-Marx-Alles;
view from the east towards Strausberger Platz.

WARSCHAUER BRÜCKE

Die erste Strecke der Berliner Stadtbahn entstand zwischen 1875 und 1882 zwischen dem Schlesischen Bahnhof (heute Ostbahnhof) und Charlottenburg für den »Localverkehr« sowie den Vorort- und Fernverkehr. Zwischen Jannowitzbrücke und Börse (heute Hackescher Markt) folgte sie den kurfürstlichen Befestigungsanlagen aus dem 17. Jahrhundert; der noch existierende Festungsgraben wurde zugeschüttet. 1923 begann man mit der Elektrifizierung des immer umfangreicher werdenden S-Bahnnetzes; Ende 1943 hatte es eine Länge von insgesamt 295 Kilometern. Nach 1945 erhielt die DDR mit der Deutschen Reichsbahn die Oberhoheit über die S-Bahn auch im Westteil der Stadt. Am 13. August 1961, dem Tag des Mauerbaus, unterbrach sie den Verkehr zwischen Ost und West, woraufhin die Westberliner zum Boykott der von Ostberlin betriebenen S-Bahn aufforderten. In den folgenden Jahrzehnten verfiel die S-Bahn im Westteil deshalb zusehends, bald mussten auch Linien stillgelegt werden. Nach 1989 begann man dann mit dem Wiederaufbau, der jedoch einige Jahre in Anspruch nahm; im Sommer 2002 konnte endlich auch wieder der S-Bahnring geschlossen werden.

The first section of the Berlin Stadtbahn was built between 1875 and 1882 from the Schlesischer Bahnhof (now Ostbahnhof) and Charlottenburg for "local traffic", and also suburban and main-line transport. It followed the lines of the 17th century princely fortifications between Jannowitzbrücke and Börse (Stock Exchange; now Hackescher Markt); the moat, which still existed, was filled in. Electrification of the ever-

expanding rail network started in 1923; by late 1943 it had an overall length of 295 kilometres. After 1945 the GDR acquired the Deutsche Reichsbahn, and with it control of the S-Bahn in the western part of the city as well. On 13 August 1961, the day the Wall was built, it also blocked traffic between East and West, so West Berlin called for a boycott of the S-Bahn, which was run by East Berlin. For this reason the S-Bahn increasingly fell into disrepair in West Berlin, and soon lines had to be closed. Reconstruction started after 1989, but it took several years; the S-Bahn ring at last became whole again in summer 2002.

S-Bahnhof Warschauer Straße, von hier aus kann man umsteigen auf die U-Bahnlinie 1 oder gelangt in den Bezirk Friedrichshain
Warschauer Strasse S-Bahn station. Here it is possible to change to U-Bahn Line 1, or get into the Friedrichshain district.

18. August 1961 am Bahnhof Zoo, Gewerkschafter fordern die Westberliner auf, die von Ostberlin betriebene S-Bahn zu boykottieren.
18 August 1961 at Bahnhof Zoo, trade unionists ask West Berliner to boycott the S-Bahn, which is run by East Berlin.

Blick von der Warschauer Brücke in Richtung Westen über das Bahngelände vor
dem Ostbahnhof.
View from Warschauer Brücke looking west over the railway land outside the
Ostbahnhof.

OBERBAUMBRÜCKE

stört, der Verkehr lief aber noch bis zum Mauerbau am 13. August 1961. Dann allerdings wurde es völlig gesperrt, da die Spree an dieser Stelle die Grenze zwischen Ost- und Westberlin bildete. 1963 richtete die DDR quer über die Brücke einen Grenzübergang ein, der von 1963 bis Ende 1989 für Fußgänger aus Westberlin in Betrieb war. Anfang der neunziger Jahre begannen umfangreiche Restaurierungsarbeiten, in deren Zusammenhang auch die seit 1945 zerstörten Türme neu erstanden. 1995 konnte die Oberbaumbrücke wieder dem Verkehr übergeben werden.

The Oberbaumbrücke takes its name from the days when access to the city was still barred by a tree-trunk – 'Baum' = 'tree' – in order to be able to check who was coming into the city and why – or to levy customs duties. Later a wooden drawbridge was erected to this end, and this splendid Berlin bridge in 1894–96. This structure in the Brandenburg brick Gothic style – the two towers are based on the towers in the Prenzlau town wall – used to include a viaduct as well as the broad carriageway. Berlin's first underground railway ran over the viaduct in 1902. The construction was badly damaged in the Second World War, but traffic still flowed until the Wall was built on 13 August 1961. But then it was stopped completely, as the Spree formed the border between East and West Berlin at this point. In 1963 the GDR built a border crossing running straight across the bridge, and this was used for pedestrians from 1963 to late 1989. Extensive restoration work started in the early nineties, and the towers, severely damaged since 1945, were included in this. The Oberbaumbrücke opened to traffic again in 1995.

Ihren Namen hat die Oberbaumbrücke noch aus der Zeit, als man mit einem Baumstamm die Zufahrt zur Stadt versperrte, um eine Kontrolle darüber zu haben, wer in die Stadt einfuhr und warum – oder um Zoll zu kassieren. Später errichtete man zu diesem Zweck eine hölzerne Zugbrücke und 1894–96 diese prächtige Berliner Brückenanlage. Zu dem Bau im Stil märkischer Backsteingotik – die beiden Türme sind denen der Stadtmauer von Prenzlau nachgebildet – gehörte schon damals neben der breiten Fahrbahn ein Viadukt, über den 1902 dann die erste U-Bahn Berlins fuhr. Im Zweiten Weltkrieg wurde das Bauwerk stark zer-

Grenzübergang Oberbaumbrücke 1984, Blick von Kreuzberg hinüber nach Friedrichshain.
Oberbaumbrücke crossing point in 1984, view from Kreuzberg over to Friedrichshain.

Blick von Friedrichshain über die Oberbaumbrücke hinüber nach Kreuzberg.
View of Friedrichshain over the Oberbaumbrücke to Kreuzberg.

Die Oberbaumbrücke verbindet die durch die Spree getrennten Stadtbezirke
Friedrichshain und Kreuzberg.
*The Oberbaumbrücke links the districts of Friedrichshain and Kreuzberg, which
are separated by the Spree.*

111

MOLECULE MAN IN TREPTOW

Wo sich der überdimensionale »Molecule Man« über dem Wasser erhebt, an der breitesten Stelle der Spree, gab es zu Zeiten der Mauer nur einen schwer bewachten Durchlass für den offiziellen Schiffsverkehr, denn das Ufer des Osthafens gehörte zur »Hauptstadt der DDR« und die andere Uferseite einige Meter flussaufwärts schon zu Westberlin. Drei Stadtbezirke begegnen sich hier: Kreuzberg, Friedrichshain und Treptow, symbolisiert durch die drei aufeinander zustrebenden Figuren Borofskys. Seit dem Fall der Mauer hat sich vieles verändert. Die »Arena«, Konzerthalle und Veranstaltungsort in einem ehemaligen Busdepot, ist zum An-

ziehungspunkt vor allem für junge Menschen geworden, ein Schwimmbecken und Cafés wie der »Freischwimmer« eröffneten auf der Kreuzberger/Treptower Seite, und an der Elsenbrücke errichtete die Allianz anstelle der früheren Elektro-Apparate-Werke ein Bürogelände mit dem 125 Meter hohem »Treptower«. Der seit 1913 bestehende Osthafen auf der Friedrichshainer Seite wird demnächst stillgelegt, das Gelände verwandelt sich in ein Berliner Medien- und Dienstleistungsviertel mit attraktiven Wohnungen in den alten Speichergebäuden.

Die Elsenbrücke im Jahr 1991; jenseits, am linken Spreeufer, die Gebäude der Elektro-Apparate-Werke, die in den dreißiger Jahren ursprünglich für die AEG gebaut wurden. Anstelle der in den neunziger Jahren abgerissenen Anlagen stehen heute von der Allianz errichtete Bürogebäude um den »Treptower« und Wohnbauten.
The Elsenbrücke in 1991. On the other side, on the left bank of the Spree, are the buildings originally built as AEG's electrical appliance factory in the thirties. These were demolished in the nineties and replaces form the Allianz office buildings around the "Treptower", and housing.

In the days of the Wall, only a heavily guarded passage for official shipping was available at the widest point of the Spree, at the point where the immense "Molecule Man" rises over the water, as the shore with the eastern harbour belonged to the "capital of the GDR", and the other bank a few metres upstream is already West Berlin. Three districts meet here: Kreuzberg, Friedrichshain and Treptow, symbolized by Borofsky's three figures striving towards each other. Much has changed since the Wall fell. The "Arena" concert hall and events location in a former bus depot has become a magnet for young people in particular, a swimming pool and cafés like the "Freischwimmer" opened on the Kreuzberg/Treptow side and Allianz have built offices in the form of the 125 metre high "Treptower" to replace the former electrical appliance factory by the Elsenbrücke. The Osthafen (east harbour) has existed since 1913 on the Friedrichshain side and will soon be closed down; the site it to be transformed into a Berlin media and services quarter with attractive dwellings in the old warehouse buildings.

Blick von der Treptower Elsenbrücke über die Spree in Richtung Zentrum. Im Vordergrund die monumentale Plastik »Molecule Man« des amerikanischen Künstlers Jonathan Borofsky.
View from the Elsenbrücke in Treptow across the Spree in the direction of the centre. In the foreground is the monumental "Molecule Man" sculpture by the American artist Jonathan Borofsky.

Zu Beginn des 20. Jahrhunderts dehnte sich Berlin in Richtung Westen aus. Am Kurfürstendamm, in Charlottenburg, Wilmersdorf und Friedenau entstanden Wohnviertel für gehobene Ansprüche, im Grunewald und in Dahlem großzügige Landhausvillen. Dort war die vornehme Welt zu Hause, für die 1907 das Kaufhaus des Westens eröffnete. Neben dem berühmten Kaufhaus Wertheim am Leipziger Platz avancierte das Haus am Wittenbergplatz bald zu einer exquisiten Adresse. Ob Stecknadel oder Modellkleid, ob Kochtopf oder Kaviar – das KaDeWe präsentierte auf seinen damals fünf Etagen ein Sortiment der Superlative. Im Jahr 1943 stürzte ein amerikanisches Flugzeug in den Lichthof und zerstörte das Gebäude fast völlig. 1950 fand die feierliche Wiedereröffnung statt, 1956 war mit der Einweihung der Lebensmittelabteilung in der sechsten Etage der Wiederaufbau abgeschlossen. Seitdem gab es mehrere Erweiterungen – eine vorläufig letzte wird 2007, zum hundertjährigen Bestehen des KaDeWe, abgeschlossen sein.

Berlin expanded westwards in the early 20th century. Exclusive residential areas came into being on the Kurfürstendamm, in Charlottenburg, Wilmersdorf and Friedenau, and spacious country villas in the Grunewald and Dahlem. This is where the elegant clientele lived that the Kaufhaus des Westens opened to serve in 1907. Along with the Wertheim department store in Leipziger Platz, the Wittenbergplatz establishment soon became a premium address. From pins to model dresses, from saucepans to caviare, – KaDeWe, on five floors at the time, presented a range of superlatives. In 1943 an American aircraft crashed in the light well and almost completely destroyed the building. It was reopened with due ceremony in 1950, and rebuilding was completed when the food hall on the sixth floor opened in 1956. Since then it has been extended several times – the last for the time being is to be completed in 2007, for KaDeWe's hundredth anniversary.

In der Fischabteilung des KaDeWe. Schon fast legendär ist der Ruf der Feinschmeckeretage. Beim Anblick des vielfältigen, exklusiven Angebots gerät jeder Genießer ins Schwärmen.
In the KaDeWe fish department. The food hall already enjoys an almost legendary reputation. Connoisseurs inevitably salivate at the sight of the varied yet exclusive produce.

Vom Wittenbergplatz aus führt die Tauentzienstraße zur Kaiser-Wilhelm-Gedächtniskirche; links das „Kadewe", um 1930.
Tauentzienstrasse leads from Wittenbergplatz to the Kaiser-Wilhelm-Gedächtniskirche; on the left is the "Kadewe" department store, c. 1930.

Das KaDeWe, das Kaufhaus des Westens am Wittenbergplatz, gehört zu den
beliebtesten Touristenattraktionen der Stadt.
*KaDeWe, the Kaufhaus des Westens in Wittenbergplatz, is one of the city's
most popular tourist attractions.*

Mit dem Ausbau des Kurfürstendamms und seiner Umgebung zu einem vornehmen Wohnviertel wurde 1891–95 die Kaiser-Wilhelm-Gedächtniskirche nach Plänen von Franz Schwechten errichtet. Die Kirche stand im Zentrum eines Bauensembles im spätromanischen Stil. Dazu gehörten der Gloriapalast an der Westseite und das Romanische Haus mit seinem berühmten Café an der Ostseite des Platzes – dort wo heute das Europa Center steht. In den zwanziger Jahren verlagerte sich das gesellschaftliche Leben der Stadt hierher in den Berliner Westen. Das Romanische Café avancierte zu einem überaus populären Treffpunkt von Künstlern und Schriftstellern; hierher kam man um zu sehen und gesehen zu werden. Nach dem Zweiten Weltkrieg gab es am Auguste-Viktoria-Platz, heute Breitscheidplatz, nur noch Trümmer, die man bis auf den Turm der Gedächtniskirche in den fünfziger Jahren abriss. Die Turmruine blieb als Mahnmal für den Zweiten Weltkrieg im Ensemble des Kirchenneubaus erhalten, der 1959–61 nach Plänen von Egon Eiermann entstand.

When the Kurfürstendamm and the surrounding area were developed as an elegant residential quarter in 1891-95 the Kaiser-Wilhelm-Gedächtniskirche was built to plans by Franz Schwechten. The church stood at the centre of a building ensemble in the late Romanesque style. This included the Gloria-Palast on the west side and the Romanisches Haus with its famous café on the east side of the square – where the Europa Center now stands. In the 1920s the city's social life shifted to the Berlin west end here. The Romanisches Café became an immensely popular rendezvous for artists and writers; people came here to see and be seen. After the Second World War there was nothing but ruins in Auguste-Viktoria-Platz, now Breitscheidplatz, and all these were pulled down in the fifties with the exception of the tower of the Gedächtniskirche. The ruined tower was retained as a memorial to the Second World War within the new church ensemble, built in 1959–61 to plans by Egon Eiermann.

Die zu Ehren Kaiser Wilhelms I. errichtete Gedächtniskirche mit ihrem 113 Meter hohen Turm, Blick von der Tauentzienstraße, Höhe Passauer Straße, im Jahr 1904.
The memorial church built in honour of Kaiser Wilhelm I, with its 113 metre high spire, view from Tauentzienstrasse at Passauer Strasse, in 1904.

Im Zentrum der City West: die Ruine der Gedächtniskirche und der Turm des Neubaus aus Glas und Beton.
In the centre of West Berlin: the ruins of the Gedächtniskirche and the tower of the new building in glass and concrete.

Der Kurfürstendamm, von den Berlinern kurz Ku'damm genannt, ist neben der Straße Unter den Linden der wohl bekannteste Boulevard der Hauptstadt. Kurfürst Joachim II. Hektor hatte hier schon 1542 einen elf Meter breiten Dammweg als Verbindung zum Jagdschloss Grunewald anlegen lassen. 1873, mit dem Ausbau Berlins zur Reichshauptstadt, verwandelte sich der Knüppeldamm auf Initiative Otto von Bismarcks in einen 53 Meter breiten Boulevard nach dem Vorbild der Champs-Elysées: mit Vorgärten, zwei Fahrbahnen, zwei Bürgersteigen, zwei Reitwegen und einer Promenade. Es entstanden luxuriös ausgestattete Wohnbauten, in denen sich das Großbürgertum und Prominente einquartierten; der Kurfürstendamm wurde zum Zentrum des vornehmen Berliner Westens. Bald zog es auch die Vergnügungsindustrie hierher, es eröffneten Theater, Restaurants, exquisite Geschäfte, Kinos. Berühmt geworden ist das Café des Westens, auch Café Größenwahn genannt. Zu Beginn des 20. Jahrhundert trafen sich dort bekannte Künstler und solche, die es werden wollten.

The Kurfürstendamm, Berliners call it Ku'damm for short, is probably the capital's best-known boulevard, with Unter den Linden. Elector (Kurfürst) Joachim II Hector had a causeway eleven metres wide built here to provide access to the Grunewald hunting lodge as early as 1542. When Berlin expanded as Reich capital in 1873, the log road was changed into a 53 metre wide boulevard modelled on the Champs Elysées on the initiative of Otto von Bismarck, with front gardens, two carriageways, two pavements, two bridle paths and a promenade. Luxurious appointed dwellings were built for the upper middle classes and eminent figures; the Kufürstendamm became the centre of the elegant west of Berlin. Soon the entertainment industry moved in here as well, theatres opened, restaurants, luxury shops and cinemas. The Café des Westens, also known as Café Grössenwahn (delusions of grandeur), became famous. Well-known artists met here in the early 20th century, along with those who wanted to be well known.

Kiosk an der Ecke Kurfürstendamm/Uhlandstraße mit der historischen Reklameschrift.
Kiosk at the Kurfüstendamm/Uhlandstrasse junction with the historic advertising typeface.

Die »Schaubühne« am Lehniner Platz. Das Gebäude wurde 1927/28 von Erich
Mendelsohn als Universum-Kino errichtet, im Zweiten Weltkrieg stark beschä-
digt und 1978–81 nach Plänen von Jürgen Sawade für das Theater umgebaut.
The "Schaubühne" in Lehniner Platz. The building was designed by Erich
Mendelsohn in 1927/28 as the Universum cinema, badly damaged in the
Second World War and converted for use as a theatre in 1978–81 to plans by
Jürgen Sawade.

121

1696–99 ließ Kurfürst Friedrich III., der sich 1701 zum ersten König in Preußen krönte, für seine Frau Sophie Charlotte vor den Toren Berlins einen Sommersitz errichten. Neben dem Dorf Lietzow baute Johann Arnold Nering die Lietzenburg, ein zweistöckiges Gebäude, das schon bald nach der Königskrönung erste Erweiterungen erfuhr. Sophie Charlotte erhob die Lietzenburg zu einem Musenhof, hier empfing sie Künstler, Musiker, Dichter, Philosophen; mit Gottfried Wilhelm Leibniz verband sie eine enge Freundschaft. Nach dem frühen Tod der Königin im Jahr 1705 ließ Friedrich I. Schloss und Dorf in Charlottenburg umbenennen, wo in den folgenden Jahrhunderten auch die nächsten Preußenkönige ihre Spuren hinterließen. Unter Friedrich dem Großen entstand der Neue Flügel mit der Goldenen Galerie und dem Konzertsaal, unter Friedrich Wilhelm II. das Belvedere im Park und Friedrich Wilhelm III. ließ sich von Schinkel direkt an der Spree den Sommerpavillon erbauen. Im Mausoleum, errichtet für die 1810 verstorbene Königin Luise, stehen auch die Sarkophage Friedrich Wilhelms III., Kaiser Wilhelms I. und seiner Frau Auguste.

Elector Friedrich III, who had himself crowned the first king of Prussia in 1701, commissioned a palace outside the gates of Berlin for his wife Sophie Charlotte in 1696–99. Johann Arnold Nering built the Lietzenburg, a two-storey building that was first extended soon after the coronation, alongside the village of Lietzow. Sophie Charlotte raised the Lietzenburg to be a palace of the muses. She received artists here, musicians, poets, philosophers; she was a close friend of Gottfried Wilhelm Leibniz. After the queen's early death in 1705, Friedrich I had the palace and village renamed Charlottenburg, and the later Prussian kings also made their mark here in subsequent centuries. The Neuer Flügel (New Wing) with the Golden Gallery and Concert Hall was added under Frederick the Great, the Belvedere in the park under Friedrich Wilhelm II and Friedrich Wilhelm III had Schinkel build him the summer pavilion directly on the Spree. The mausoleum, built for Queen Luise who died in 1810, contains the sarcophaguses of Friedrich Wilhelm III, Kaiser Wilhelm I and his wife Auguste.

An die reizvolle barocke Gartenanlage im Charlottenburger Schlosspark, die in den letzten Jahren mit viel Liebe zum Detail nach alten Musterbüchern wieder hergerichtet wurde, schließt sich ein weitläufiger Landschaftsgarten an.
There is an extensive landscape garden attached to the charming baroque gardens in the Charlottenburg park, which has been restored in recent years following old pattern books, with loving attention to detail.

Der Ehrenhof des Schlosses Charlottenburg mit dem Reiterstandbild des Großen
Kurfürsten von Andreas Schlüter. Die barocke Anlage ist die größte und auch die
bekannteste der in Berlin erhaltenen Schlösser.
*The court d'honneur in Charlottenburg Palace with the equestrian statue of the
Great Elector by Andreas Schlüter. This baroque complex is the largest and also
the best-known of Berlin's surviving palaces.*

123

Mit seinen 138 Metern Höhe ist der Funkturm auf dem Ausstellungs- und Messegelände in Charlottenburg eines der Wahrzeichen Berlins und zugleich ein Zeugnis aus der Pionierzeit des Rundfunks. Begonnen wurde mit seinem Bau anlässlich der ersten Großen Deutschen Funkausstellung im Jahr 1924, zwei Jahre später, zur dritten Funkausstellung, fand seine feierliche Einweihung statt. Die Rede zur Eröffnung hielt kein Geringerer als Albert Einstein. Der Turm, den der Architekt Heinrich Straumer nach dem Vorbild des Pariser Eiffelturms entwarf, war zunächst nur als Antennenträger für den 1923 in Berlin begründeten deutschen Hörfunk geplant, erhielt dann aber noch eine Aussichtsplattform und ein 55 Meter hoch gelegenes Restaurant. Auch nach dem Zweiten Weltkrieg diente der Turm bis 1962 der Funk- und Fernsehübertragung. 1966 wurde er unter Denkmalschutz gestellt; seit 1967 gibt es zu seinen Füßen das Deutsche Rundfunkmuseum.

The 138 metre Funkturm (Radio Tower) on the exhibition and trade fair site in Charlottenburg is a famous Berlin landmark and at the same time evidence of the early days of radio. Construction started for the Great German Radio Exhibition in 1924, and the opening ceremony took place two years later, for the third radio exhibition. The opening speech was made by no less than Albert Einstein. The tower, modelled by architect Heinrich Straumer on the Eiffel Tower in Paris, was first of all intended simply to carry the aerial for the German radio station founded in Berlin in 1923, but then acquired an viewing platform, and a restaurant at 55 metres. It was used for radio an television broadcasts even after the Second World War, until 1962. It was listed in 1966, and the German Radio Museum has been at its feet since 1967.

Das nach Entwürfen des Architekten Hans Poelzig 1931 fertig gestellte Haus des Rundfunks an der Masurenallee war eines der ersten Funkhäuser in Deutschland. Das Foto wurde im April 1931 vom Funkturm aufgenommen.
The Haus des Rundfunks in Masurenallee, completed to designs by the architect Hans Poelzig in 1931, was one of the first radio stations in Germany. The photograph was taken from the Funkturm in April 1931.

Der Funkturm am Messegelände, davor die 18 Meter hohe und 50 Meter lange Skulptur »Looping« von Ursula Sax.
The Funkturm (Radio Tower) at the Exhibition Centre, in front is Ursula Sax's "Looping" sculpture, 18 metres high and 50 metres long.

Der Funkturm und das 1973–79 nach Plänen der Architekten Ralph Schüler und Ursulina Schüler-Witte errichtete Internationale Congress Centrum (ICC), von dem ein Fußgängerübergang über den Messedamm zum Messegelände führt. Vorn links erkennt man die von Jean Ipoustéguy geschaffene Bronzeskulptur »Ecbatane – Der Mensch baut seine Stadt«.

The Funkturm and the International Congress Centre, built from 1973–79 to plans by the architects Ralph Schüler and Ursulina Schüler-Witte, from which a pedestrian walkway leads over the Messedamm to the exhibition centre. Front left is the bronze sculpture "Ecbatane – Man builds his city", by Jean Ipoustéguy.

Zu den XI. Olympischen Spielen 1936 entstand auf dem ehemaligen Reichssportfeld 1934–36 nach Plänen des Architekten Werner March das Berliner Olympiastadion. Unter der Leitung des Hamburger Architekturbüros von Gerkan, Marg & Partner wurde es zwischen 2000 und 2004 einer umfangreichen, denkmalgerechten Sanierung und Modernisierung unterzogen. Das Stadion ist der zentrale Ort eines ausgedehnten Olympiageländes mit verschiedenen Sportstätten. Dazu gehört das Maifeld, nach den Spielen von 1936 ein Aufmarsch- und Appellplatz der Nationalsozialisten. Während der Teilung der Stadt – nach dem Zweiten Weltkrieg gehörte das Gelände zum britischen Sektor – veranstalteten die Briten auf dem Maifeld unter anderem Poloturniere und die alljährliche Geburtstagsparade zu Ehren Königin Elisabeths II. Nach Westen hin wird das Maifeld vom monumentalen Glockenturm und der dazugehörigen Gedenkhalle begrenzt. Vom Turm, der im Zweiten Weltkrieg stark zerstört, 1963 aber wieder aufgebaut wurde, hat man einen fantastischen Rundblick über die Stadt, den Grunewald und die Havelseen.

The Berlin Olympic Stadium was built on the former Reichssportfeld in 1934–36 for the 1936 Olympic Games, to plans by the architect Werner March. It was extensively refurbished and modernized under the direction of the Hamburg architecture practice von Gerkan, Marg & Partner between 2000 and 2004, consistently with its listed status. The stadium

is the central feature of an extensive Olympic site with various sports facilities. They include the Maifeld, which the National Socialists used as a parade and inspection ground after the 1936 games. While the city was divided – the site was part of the British sector after the Second World War – the British used to arrange polo tournaments among other things on the Maifeld, and the annual birthday parade in honour of Queen Elizabeth II. The Maifeld is bordered on the western side by the monumental bell tower and the memorial hall attached to it. The tower was badly damaged in the Second World War, but rebuilt in 1963. It affords a fantastic panorama over the city, the Grunewald and the Havel lakes.

Haupteingang an der Ostseite des Olympiastadions, dessen neues Dach hier erkennbar ist. Überraschend für die Zuschauer nach dem Umbau war auch die neue, hertha-blaue Tartanbahn des Stadions.
Main entrance on the east side of the Olympic Stadium, whose new roof can be seen here. The stadium's new tartan running track in Hertha BSC blue also surprised spectators after the conversion.

Das Berliner Olympiastadion ist das Heimstadion der Bundesliga-Mannschaft Hertha BSC und ihrer Fußballfans.
The Berlin Olympic Stadium is the home stadium for the Bundesliga team Hertha BSC and its football fans.

Das neue Dach über dem umgebauten Olympiastadion, Ort des Endspiels der
Fußball-Weltmeisterschaft 2006. Etwa 75 000 Zuschauer finden hier Platz.
The new roof over the converted Olympic Stadium, the location for the 2006
World Cup final. The stadium seats about 75,000 spectators.

Als »verfallenes römisches Landhaus« ließ Friedrich Wilhelm II. 1794 – 97 das kleine Schloss auf der Pfaueninsel für sich und seine Geliebte Wilhelmine Encke errichten.
Friedrich Wilhelm II had the little palace on the Pfaueninsel built for himself and his mistress Wilhelmine Encke in 1794 – 97, as a "dilapidated Roman country house".

Nur zu Fuß und über eine Fähre erreicht man die vom Wasser der Havel umgebene Pfaueninsel im Südwesten der Stadt. Zur Zeit des Großen Kurfürsten, als die Insel noch Kaninchenwerder hieß, hatte hier der »Goldmacher« Johannes Kunckel sein Domizil; für den brandenburgischen Herrscher stellte er wertvolles Rubinglas her. Mehr als hundert Jahre später ließ Preußenkönig Friedrich Wilhelm II. die Insel als Ausflugsort für sich und seine Geliebte herrichten, denn von seinem Marmorpalais in Potsdam konnte er die hübsche Gegend mit einem Boot gut erreichen. Sein Nachfolger Friedrich Wilhelm III. vertrieb zwar die Geliebte seines Vaters, das Eiland mit den romantischen Bauten aber wusste auch er zu schätzen. Das 67 Hektar große Gelände ließ er vom Gartenkünstler Peter Joseph Lenné gestalten und siedelte in Gehegen und Häusern eine große Zahl exotischer Tiere an. 1845 wurden die meisten von ihnen dem neu gegründeten Zoologischen Garten übergeben. Lediglich die Pfauen erinnern noch an die königliche Menagerie.

The Pfaueninsel (Peacock Island) in the south-west of the city is surrounded by the waters of the Havel and can only be reached on foot and by ferry. At the time of the Great Elector, when the island was still called Kaninchenwerder, the "Goldmacher" (alchemist) Johannes Kunckel had made it his domicile; he produced valuable ruby glass for the ruler of Brandenburg. Over a hundred years later the Prussian king Friedrich Wilhelm II had the island made into a place he could visit with his mistress, as it was easy for him to reach the pretty area by boat from his marble palace in Potsdam. His successor Friedrich Wilhelm III got rid of his father's mistress, but he too was fond of the island with its romantic buildings. He had the garden artist Peter Joseph Lenné design the 67 hectare site, and moved in a large number of exotic animals, which were kept in enclosures and houses. Most of them were presented to the newly founded Zoological Gardens in 1845. Only the peacocks still provide a reminder of the royal menagerie.

Das Kavaliershaus auf der Pfaueninsel entstand 1824–26 nach Plänen Schinkels; die Fassade schmückte einst ein gotisches Haus in Danzig.
The Kavaliershaus on the Pfaueninsel was built in 1824–26 to plans by Schinkel; the façade once adorned a Gothic house in Danzig.

Der Schlosspark Glienicke liegt direkt an der Berlin–Potsdamer Chaussee, mit deren Bau 1790 begonnen wurde. Das Gut, nun sehr verkehrsgünstig zwischen den beiden Residenzen gelegen, erwarb der preußische Staatsmann Karl August Fürst von Hardenberg. Er beauftragte 1816 den noch kaum bekannten Gärtner Peter Joseph Lenné mit der Neugestaltung seines Gutsgartens, eine Arbeit, die Lenné unter dem neuen Besitzer Prinz Carl von Preußen nach dem Tod Hardenbergs 1822 fortsetzte. Der Bruder Friedrich Wilhelms III. träumte von einer italienischen Landschaft auf märkischem Sand und engagierte dafür auch die Architekten Schinkel und Ludwig Persius. Aus dem Landhaus wurde ein klar gegliedertes klassizistisches Schloss, aus dem Billardhaus das Kasino, und im Park errichtete Persius ein Maschinenhaus und eine Orangerie. Durch das ideale Zusammenspiel von Gartenkunst und Architektur ist eine einzigartige Landschaft entstanden, die zu einem wichtigen Bestandteil der Potsdamer Kulturlandschaft avancierte.

The Glienicke Schlosspark is placed directly on the main Berlin-Potsdam road, which was constructed from 1790 onwards. The estate was now situated very conveniently between the two residences in terms of transport, and was acquired by the Prussian statesman Prince Karl August von Hardenberg. In 1816 he commissioned the gardener Peter Joseph Lenné, who was scarcely known at the time, to redesign his estate garden, a job that Lenné continued under the new owner Prince Carl of Prussia after Hardenberg died in 1822. Friedrich Wilhelm II's brother dreamed of an Italian landscape on the sand of Brandenburg, and engaged the architects Schinkel and Ludwig Persius to work on it as well. The country house became a lucidly articulated neo-classical palace, the billiard building became the Kasino and Persius built a machine house and an orangery in the park. The ideal interplay of horticulture and architecture created a unique landscape that came to be an important component of the Potsdam culture landscape.

Das Kasino am Ufer der Havel im Glienicker Park erbaute Schinkel 1824/25 für Prinz Carl von Preußen.
Schinkel built the Kasino on the bank of the Havel in the Glienicke Park for Prince Carl of Prussia in 1825/25.

Eine der beiden Löwenfontänen des Brunnens vor dem Schloss Glienicke. Die 1835–37 von Schinkel errichtete Anlage entstand nach einem Vorbild in der Villa Medici in Rom.
One of the two lion fountains on the well outside Schloss Glienicke. The palace was built by Schinkel in 1835-37 and was modelled on the Villa Medici in Rome.

Blick über die Glienicker Brücke zum Glienicker Park. Zur Zeit der Mauer verlief
hier die Grenze zwischen Westberlin und Potsdam, das zur DDR gehörte. Die
Brücke war einer der legendären Orte während der Zeit des Kalten Krieges, hier
tauschten die Sowjetunion und die Westalliierten ihre vom Gegner enttarnten
Spione aus.
*View over the Glienicke Bridge to the Glienicke Park. In the days of the Wall the
border between West Berlin and Potsdam, which belonged to the GDR, passed
through here. The bridge was a legendary location during the Cold War. The Soviet Union and the Western Allies used to swap spies unmasked by the enemy
here.*

CITY OF ARCHITECTURAL SOLITAIRES by Andreas Krause

The sky is deep blue, the light hard and clear, not at all typical of Berlin. From the left, Alexander Calder's free-standing sculpture pushes its way into the picture, from the right the Neue Nationalgalerie (New National Gallery), an audacious construction of steel supports and glass walls. The only building Mies van der Rohe designed in Germany after emigrating, the gallery has been called the "Parthenon of the twentieth century". But in an apparently empty space at the centre of the shot, as if the lines of the paving stones had always been stretching towards it, rises the St.-Matthäus-Kirche (St Matthew's Church), built in 1844 by August Stüler. Its plain façade, horizontally articulated by coloured bands of brick, its round-arched windows, the three apses – these are not nineteenth-century inventions but borrowings from the architecture of the early Christian period. In Berlin, this interlocking of styles and epochs is anything but uncommon, yet it's only the gaze of the photographer Erik-Jan Ouwerkerk that presents the architectural ensemble from an ideal angle.

Severely damaged in the Second World War, the exterior of the St.-Matthäus-Kirche was rebuilt in 1959/60 in its original form. The interior is a perfectly unadorned space dominated by concrete beams. Once surrounded by dense residential development, the "yellow eminence" today contrasts vividly with the expressive buildings of the Kulturforum (Cultural Forum) around it. Ouwerkerk's photograph is a kind of bridge: what we see originates in the nineteenth and twentieth century, but our viewpoint is more recent. The arrangement could be interpreted as making an architectural monument of the Prussian capital push aside an epitome of modernism, even if the latter does still determine the perspective. That kind of interpretation would have been unthinkable ten years ago – but then again, ten years ago nobody would have seriously considered reconstructing Berlin's Stadtschloss (City Palace), the Hohenzollern residence, demolished in 1950, which for many centuries had been the focal point of the old double city Berlin-Cölln. This is where the city's architectural history began, a history whose testimonies are collected in this volume.

The centre of Berlin was once a "hill surrounded by water and marshland" – that, at least, is the meaning of the Wendic kolln from which the name "Cölln" derives. Cölln was a settlement that arose on the island on the River Spree and received its charter from Brandenburg in the early thirteenth century. The economic development of Cölln, in tandem with Berlin on the opposite bank of the river, benefited from an ancient trade route connecting the rivers Elbe and Oder, which here

crossed the Spree at a narrow place. The double city, administered in two parts as late as 1709, prospered under the Ascanian and Bavarian margraves. It became a meeting-place for the guilds of the central Mark, a member of the Hanseatic League and, after acquiring jurisdiction in 1391, an independent city.

Berlin's architectural history might be narrated as the history of its fortifications. That's not just because the medieval city walls ran right across the square where the Stadtschloss later stood, or because new walls were built during waves of expansion like those under the Great Elector and the "Soldier King" Frederick William I. There was a defensive intent, as well, in the building of the Electors' castle, begun in 1448. The castle, which later became the Stadtschloss, was designed to provide protection both from external enemies and from the Berliners themselves, who tried in vain to sabotage the building site through flooding. There were opponents to the building of a Stadtschloss even in those days. Yet the Berliners might have been grateful to the Hohenzollern dynasty, which was granted the Brandenburg Mark by Emperor Sigismund in 1411. The burgrave and imperial prince Frederick VI of Nuremberg, a man of both action and financial muscle, began his reign by putting a violent end to the devastations of robber barons like the Quitzows, which were threatening to destroy Berlin's commercial traffic. However, when his successor Frederick II (1437–1470) claimed sovereign rights over city property, that outbreak of the notorious "Berlin discontent" was the result. Though unable to prevent the castle being built, the townspeople paid dearly for their actions, losing a large part of their assets and city privileges.

This was the beginning of an era that only ended in 1918 with the abdication of William II. By the early seventeenth century, the sister cities had grown into an important centre of trade for the Brandenburg and central German region. After the Thirty Years War, which almost halved the population from 14,000 to 7,500, Berlin expanded into a fortified city. Even before the Elector of Brandenburg, Frederick III, was crowned King Frederick I in Prussia in 1701, the royal residence had begun to stretch westwards when the Great Elector laid out the boulevard Unter den Linden, originally as a lime-tree avenue. The new pattern of urban design had been established, and the grid plan of the Friedrichstadt and Dorotheenstadt quarters, their streets seeming to stretch into infinity, has remained in place until the present day.

There are many other reminders of the vigorous building activity in the reigns of Frederick I and Frederick II: the Zeughaus (Arsenal) by Johann

DIE STADT DER SOLITÄRE von Andreas Krause

Der Himmel ist tiefblau, das Licht hart und klar, ganz untypisch für Berlin. Von links schiebt sich das Stabile Alexander Calders ins Bild, von rechts die Neue Nationalgalerie, eine kühne Konstruktion aus Stahlstützen und Glaswänden. »Parthenon des 20. Jahrhunderts« hat man ihn genannt, den einzigen Bau Mies van der Rohes, der nach seiner Emigration in Deutschland ent-stand. In der Bildmitte aber, als würden die Fugen der Bodenplatten schon immer auf sie zustreben, erhebt sich wie auf freiem Feld die 1844 von August Stüler erbaute St.-Matthäus-Kirche. Ihre schlichte, durch farbige Ziegelbänder waagerecht gegliederte Fassade, die Rundbogenfenster, die drei Apsiden, das alles sind keine Erfindungen des 19. Jahrhunderts, sondern Entlehnungen aus der Architektur frühchristlicher Zeit. Eine solche Verschränkung der Stile und Epochen ist in Berlin nicht eben selten, doch erst der Blick des Fotografen Erik-Jan Ouwerkerk stellt dieses städtebauliche Ensemble in einer geradezu idealen Ansicht vor.

Im Zweiten Weltkrieg schwer beschädigt, wurde die St.-Matthäus-Kirche 1959/60 in ihrer äußeren Form wiederhergestellt. Innen ist sie ein ganz schmuckloser, von Betonträgern dominierter Raum. Einst von dichter Wohnbebauung umgeben, steht die »gelbe Eminenz« heute in starkem Kontrast zu den expressiven Häusern des Kulturforums.

Ouwerkerks Fotografie ist eine Brücke: Was wir sehen, stammt aus dem 19. und 20. Jahrhundert, der Standpunkt des Betrachters aber ist jüngeren Datums. Diese Motivanordnung auf dem Bild so zu deuten, dass ein Baudenkmal der preußischen Hauptstadt ein Inbild der Moderne an den Rand drängt, auch wenn dieses weiterhin die Perspektive vorgibt – eine solche Interpretation wäre noch vor zehn Jahren undenkbar gewesen. Vor zehn Jahren hätte man aber auch nicht den Wiederaufbau des Berliner Schlosses ernsthaft erwägen können, jener 1950 gesprengten Hohenzollernresidenz, die jahrhundertelang der Mittelpunkt der ehemaligen Doppelstadt Berlin-Cölln war. Hier begann die Baugeschichte der Stadt, deren Zeugnisse dieser Band versammelt.

Die Mitte Berlins war einst ein »von Sumpf und Wasser umgebener Hügel« – jedenfalls ist das die Bedeutung des wendischen Wortes »Kollen«, von dem sich der Name »Cölln« ableitet. So hieß die auf der Spreeinsel entstandene Siedlung, die im frühen 13. Jahrhundert das brandenburgische Stadtrecht erhielt. Die gemeinsame wirtschaftliche Entwicklung Cöllns und des am östlichen Flussufer gelegenen Berlin profitierte von einem alten, Elbe und Oder verbindenden Handelsweg, der hier an einer günstigen Stelle die Spree kreuzte. Die Doppelstadt, noch bis 1709 getrennt verwaltet, gedieh bereits unter den askanischen und bayerischen Markgrafen, wurde Versammlungsort der mittelmärkischen Stände, Mitglied der Hanse und selbständig durch den Erwerb der Gerichtsbarkeit 1391.

Die Baugeschichte Berlins ließe sich als die Geschichte seiner Befestigungen erzählen. Dies nicht nur, weil die mittelalterliche Stadtmauer quer über den späteren Schlossplatz verlief oder wesentliche Stadterweiterungen wie unter dem Großen Kurfürsten und dem Soldatenkönig neue Stadtmauern zur Folge hatten. Auch der 1448 begonnene Bau der kurfürstlichen Burg, aus der später das Berliner Schloss hervorging, diente dem Schutz – dem Schutz vor äußeren Feinden, aber auch vor den Berlinern selbst, die vergeblich versuchten, den Bauplatz unter Wasser zu setzen. Schlossgegner gab es schon damals.

Dabei konnten die Berliner dem Geschlecht der Hohenzollern, das 1411 von König Sigmund mit der Mark Brandenburg belehnt wurde, eigentlich ganz dankbar sein. Tat- und finanzkräftig wie er war, machte Burggraf und Reichsfürst Friedrich VI. von Nürnberg erst einmal dem märkischen Raubrittertum derer von Quitzow ein gewaltsames Ende; es hatte auch den Berliner Handelsverkehr fast zum Erliegen gebracht. Als aber sein Nachfolger Friedrich II. (1437–1470) landesherrliches Eigentum für sich beanspruchte, das im Besitz der Stadt war, kam es zu jenem gewalttätigen Ausbruch »Berliner Unwillens«, der allerdings den Bau der Burg nicht verhindern konnte, dafür die Bürger einen Großteil ihres Vermögens und ihrer städtischen Privilegien kostete.

Das war der Anfang einer geschichtlichen Periode, die erst 1918, mit der Abdankung Kaiser Wilhelm II., zu Ende ging. Bis zum frühen 17. Jahrhundert gediehen die Schwesterstädte zu einem bedeutenden Handelszentrum im brandenburgisch-mitteldeutschen Raum. Nach dem Dreißigjährigen Krieg, der die Einwohnerzahl von 14 000 auf 7 500 fast halbierte, wurde Berlin zur Festungsstadt ausgebaut. Noch bevor Friedrich III./I. 1701 die preußische Königswürde erlangte, begann die Residenz nach Westen auszustrahlen, mit der vom Großen Kurfürsten als Plantage angelegten Straße Unter den Linden. Das neue Muster des Städtebaus, der rasterartige Grundriss mit den sich schier im Unendlichen verlierenden Straßenfluchten der Friedrich- und der Dorotheenstadt hat sich bis heute erhalten.

Ebenfalls erhalten sind viele Zeugnisse der regen Bautätigkeit unter Friedrich I. und Friedrich II.: das Zeughaus von Johann Arnold Nering, Martin Grünberg, Andreas Schlüter (Masken der sterbenden Krieger) und Jean de Bodt, das Opernhaus von Georg Wenzeslaus von Knobelsdorff, das Palais des Prinzen Heinrich (heute Humboldt-Universität) und

Arnold Nering, Martin Grünberg, Andreas Schlüter (who carved the line of dying warriors) and Jean de Bodt; and at the Forum Fridericianum the opera house by Georg Wenzeslaus von Knobelsdorff, Prince Henry's palace (today the Humboldt University), the Hedwigskirche (St Hedwig's Cathedral) by Johannes Boumann and the Königliche Bibliothek (Royal Library) by Georg Christian Unger and Boumann's son Georg Friedrich. With its great curved façade, the Library is a masterpiece of Frederician baroque.

Anyone who has ever tried to summon up an impression of old Berlin will have come to the melancholy conclusion that very little of it is left. Yet in view of the damage caused by bombing in the Second World War, it's actually surprising how much has been preserved: the Schauspielhaus (the former royal playhouse), the Friedrichwerder Church or Charlottenburg palace, once listed for demolition, are just a few examples. Certainly, the palace at Charlottenburg was more seriously damaged than the "palace at Cölln", the Stadtschloss, which was demolished chiefly for political reasons. But it was not only the city's eastern half that suffered from the craze for demolition; even in the West, in general urban planners were anything but sensitive in their treatment of the historical building stock.

The "large-scale development of Berlin into a metropolis", as noted in 1937 by the urban historian Friedrich Kuntze, was not an idea new to the post-war period. It had already been planned by the Nazis. On the bend in the River Spree and at today's Kulturforum, they began the demolition of imperial Berlin, aiming to clear space for the new world capital "Germania" with its gigantic public buildings; the job was finished by Allied bombing raids. After the War the old government buildings – the palaces of the Reich president and Reich chancellor, the palace of Prince Albert – in Wilhelmstrasse, a street even Hitler had despised, were demolished on both sides of the zone border, even though almost all of them would have been capable of reconstruction. Hans Scharoun built the Neue Staatsbibliothek (New State Library) right in the middle of Alte Potsdamer Strasse, what used to be autobahn number 1 from Aachen to Königsberg, leading to Potsdamer Platz via today's Marlene-Dietrich-Platz. And when the Hohenzollern Stadtschloss was blasted by the Soviet occupation forces, it was just the sad culmination of a will to amnesia that affected both halves of Germany and crossed the boundaries of epochs.

Fortunately, other days were to come. The change in the climate of opinion might be dated from the restoration of Christian Daniel Rauch's equestrian monument to Frederick the Great, in 1980. The statue had been walled in until 1950, and survived the subsequent decades in a shed at Sanssouci, Potsdam. Looking back, it was probably a sign of the gradual inner collapse of East Germany that, in its final period, the country returned to its Prussian heritage – though to East Germany's credit, it had already finished reconstructing Unter den Linden and the Gendarmenmarkt piazza, with Karl Friedrich Schinkel's Schauspielhaus and the imposing turreted churches by Carl von Gontard.

In 2001 urgently necessary restoration work was completed and the monument to Frederick the Great was moved back to its historical location on Unter den Linden, near Bebelplatz. It is said that on the spot where the sculpture now stands, Electress Dorothea once planted the first of Unter den Linden's lime-trees; here, too, was the triumphal arch that welcomed the young Queen Louise of Prussia into Berlin. Only Rauch's marble statues of generals Bülow and Scharnhorst still await attention. The plan is to return them to their old place outside the Neue Wache (New Guardhouse), along with the statues of field marshals Gneisenau, Blücher and Yorck von Wartenburg, which at present stand forlornly "like colossal garden gnomes on the lawn" (Tilmann Buddensieg) between the opera house and the opera café. If East Germany had taken early action on these statues too, the reunified city would have been saved much anguished and fruitless debate.

The late eighteenth century saw further architectural change. Carl Gotthard Langhans' Brandenburg Gate became the symbol of the longing for a middle-class, intellectual "Athens on the Spree". Soon after, between 1816 and 1835, Karl Friedrich Schinkel created the epitomes of "Prussian style" neo-classical Berlin: the Neue Wache, the Altes Museum (Old Museum), the Bauakademie (Architecture Academy), the Friedrichwerder Church. These buildings show particularly clearly how Berlin was transforming itself into a bourgeois city. The basic forms of industrial architecture were already being developed by Schinkel, for example in designs for a large department store on Unter den Linden or for urban expansion in Moabit and Köpenicker Feld (today Kreuzberg). The influence of Schinkel's ideas continued well into the second half of the nineteenth century.

As new districts began to be built outside the ancient city walls and customs boundaries, property speculation flourished. In 1853 the Berlin police building regulations, laying down minimum fire safety standards, had paved the way for standardised street-edge block developments of rented housing: tenement blocks had to have an inner courtyard exactly

die Hedwigskirche von Johannes Boumann sowie die Königliche Bibliothek (»Kommode«) von Georg Christian Unger und Boumanns Sohn Georg Friedrich am Forum Fridericianum – mit ihrer kurvig zurückspringenden Fassade ein Hauptwerk des friderizianischen Barock.

Hat man einmal versucht, sich eine Vorstellung vom alten Berlin zu machen, kann man nur wehmütig zur Kenntnis nehmen, wie wenig davon noch erhalten ist. Hält man sich aber die Schäden vor Augen, die die Stadt im Bombenkrieg erlitten hat, ist es erstaunlich, wie viel gerettet wurde: sei es das Schauspielhaus, die Friedrichwerdersche Kirche oder das einst für den Abriss vorgesehene Schloss Charlottenburg, um nur wenige Beispiele zu nennen. Zugegeben, Letzteres war schwerer getroffen worden als das Schloss »zu Cölln«, dessen Zerstörung vorwiegend politisch motiviert war. Aber die Abrissbirne schlug nicht nur im Osten ein; generell gingen die Stadtplaner mit dem historischen Bestand auch im Westen nicht gerade zimperlich um.

Der »großzügige Ausbau Berlins zur Weltstadt«, den der Stadthistoriker Friedrich Kuntze 1937 feststellte, war nicht erst eine Idee der Nachkriegszeit, sondern schon ein Plan der Nationalsozialisten. Am Spreebogen und am heutigen Kulturforum hatte bereits die Demolierung des kaiserlichen Berlin begonnen, um Platz zu schaffen für die Welthauptstadt »Germania« mit ihren gigantischen Repräsentationsbauten – der Luftkrieg besorgte dann den Rest. Die alten Regierungsbauten in der schon von Hitler verschmähten Wilhelmstraße – Reichspräsidentenpalais, Reichskanzlerpalais oder Palais des Prinzen Albrecht – wurden, obwohl fast alle zum Wiederaufbau geeignet, beiderseits der Zonengrenze abgerissen. Hans Scharoun errichtete die Neue Staatsbibliothek mitten auf der Alten Potsdamer Straße, der ehemaligen Reichsstraße 1 von Aachen nach Königsberg, die über den heutigen Marlene-Dietrich-Platz zum Potsdamer Platz führte. Die Sprengung des Hohenzollernschlosses war da nur der traurige Höhepunkt einer durchaus gesamtdeutschen – und die Epochen übergreifenden – Selbstvergessenheit.

Zum Glück kamen andere Zeiten. Symbol für den geistigen Wandel mag die 1980 erfolgte Wiederaufstellung des Reiterdenkmals Friedrich des Großen von Christian Daniel Rauch sein, welches, bis 1950 eingemauert, die folgenden Jahrzehnte in einem Bretterverschlag in Sanssouci überstanden hatte. Rückblickend betrachtet war es wohl ein Zeichen für die innere Auszehrung der DDR, dass sie sich in ihrer Spätzeit noch dem preußischen Erbe zuwandte – um den Wiederaufbau der »Linden« und die Rekonstruktion des Gendarmenmarktes mit Karl Friedrich Schinkels Schauspielhaus und den imposanten Turmbauten

Carl von Gontards hatte man sich allerdings auch vorher schon verdient gemacht.

Das Reiterdenkmal Friedrich des Großen jedenfalls wurde 2001 nach dringend erforderlicher Restaurierung an seinen historischen Ort auf der Höhe des Bebelplatzes verlegt. Dort, wo es heute steht, soll Kurfürstin Dorothea den ersten Baum der Straße Unter den Linden gepflanzt haben, und hier hatte auch die Triumphpforte beim Einzug der jungen Königin Luise in Berlin gestanden. Nur die von Rauch geschaffenen Marmorstandbilder der Generäle Bülow und Scharnhorst warten noch darauf, wieder vor der Neuen Wache aufgestellt zu werden, wie auch die Standbilder der Feldmarschälle Gneisenau, Blücher und Yorck von Wartenburg, die sich derzeit »wie kolossale Gartenzwerge im Grünen« (Tilmann Buddensieg) zwischen Staatsoper und Opern-Café verlieren. Hätte die DDR auch hier gehandelt, wäre der wiedervereinigten Stadt manch quälend fruchtlose Diskussion erspart geblieben.

Am Ende des 18. Jahrhunderts kam es erneut zu Veränderungen in der Baukunst. Das Brandenburger Tor von Carl Gotthard Langhans wurde zum Symbol der Sehnsucht nach einem bürgerlich-intellektuellen »Spree-Athen«. Bald darauf, zwischen 1816 und 1835, schuf Karl Friedrich Schinkel die Inbilder des klassizistischen Berlin im »preußischen« Stil, die Neue Wache, das Alte Museum, die Bauakademie, die Friedrichwerdersche Kirche. In diesen Bauten wurde der Wandel zu einer bürgerlichen Stadt besonders deutlich. Die bereits von Schinkel entwickelten Grundformen industriellen Bauens, etwa für ein großes Kaufhaus Unter den Linden, aber auch seine Stadterweiterungspläne für Moabit und das Köpenicker Feld (das heutige Kreuzberg) wirkten weit in die 2. Hälfte des 19. Jahrhunderts hinein.

Mit den neuen Vierteln jenseits der alten Stadt- und Zollmauern blühte auch die Bodenspekulation, seit 1853 die Berliner Baupolizeiordnung mit ihren brandschutztechnischen Minimalforderungen die Mietskasernenviertel ermöglichte: Ein Hinterhof musste gerade so groß sein, dass die Feuerspritze wenden konnte. 1862 trat der Hobrechtsche Bebauungsplan für Berlin und Charlottenburg in Kraft und ließ ringförmig die »größte Mietskasernenstadt der Welt« entstehen. Die Einwohnerzahl des Großraums Berlin verdreifachte sich zwischen 1871 und 1900 von 900 000 auf 2,7 Millionen.

Die typische Alt-Berliner Wohnstraße mit den engen, dunklen Höfen entstand meist zwischen 1880 und 1920. Auch die Idee der Gartenstadt, aufgekommen zwischen den Weltkriegen, hat die Beliebtheit der traditionellen Mietskaserne, bei allen ihren Nachteilen, nicht geschmälert:

passer-by in front of Frederick the Great's monument at night, the placard on the lamp-post in front of the Royal Library. These subtle allusions evoke the impression of a strongly muffled urban life, as if far-off noises were seeping through a thick pane of glass.

At first glance these pictures may seem to have very little to do with a vibrant metropolis. But by puzzling the viewer, these unexcited, almost static views force him to confront his own images of Berlin, and thus ultimately capture something very typical of the city. For Berlin's special quality is to be found not on the aesthetic but the intellectual level. "The distinctions of Berlin," noted the writer Martin Kessel in 1959, "consist in its huge number of openly displayed questions." To enter into dialogue with those is the Berliner's real challenge: "Berlin is a Socratic city. The very fact that it forces each individual to confront it as an idea and a phenomenon is Socratic. One comes to Berlin not so much to look at it as to reach a judgement on it. However, no-one should forget that the spirit of Berlin is dialectical and paradoxical, always at once the opposite of its own opposite, and that anyone who undertakes to judge it will not escape characterising himself as well." Berlin's fluid and "becoming" aspect, all too long regarded as part of its architectural history, in fact applies more to the experience of the inhabitants and visitors, who are constantly faced with new questions and discoveries. Take the building site fence that encloses the ruined portico of Anhalter Bahnhof station, what Walter Benjamin called the "womb of the railway" – does it connote reconstruction or demolition? When the building, with its bold glass and iron roof, was blasted in 1961, a void was left that only began to be filled after the construction of the new Tempodrom. Here, too, old and new interlock in an unexpected and provocative way. In the end, this city's contradictory solitaires do generate a coherent picture that is more than the sum of its parts – but why that should be so remains a very open question.

Fragwürdigkeiten.« Mit ihnen sich auseinanderzusetzen sei die eigentliche Herausforderung des Berliners: »Berlin ist eine sokratische Stadt. Allein die Tatsache, dass es jeden zwingt, sich mit ihm als Idee und Phänomen auseinanderzusetzen, ist bereits sokratisch. Man kommt weniger nach Berlin, um es anzuschauen, als vielmehr, um sich ein Urteil darüber zu bilden. Nur sollte man nicht vergessen, dass der Geist Berlins dialektisch und paradox und stets auch das Gegenteil seines Gegenteils ist und dass derjenige, der sich bemüßigt fühlt, es zu beurteilen, sich dadurch auch selbst charakterisiert«.

Das Fließende und Werdende Berlins, das man allzu lange in der Baugeschichte der Stadt erblickte – damit sind viel eher die Erlebnisse der Bewohner und Besucher beschrieben, die mit immer neuen Fragen und Entdeckungen konfrontiert werden. Der Bauzaun, der die Portikusruine des Anhalter Bahnhofs umschließt, der »Mutterhöhle der Eisenbahn« (Walter Benjamin) – weckt er die Assoziation von Wiederaufbau oder Abriss? Die Sprengung des Gebäudes mit seiner kühnen Dachkonstruktion aus Glas und Eisen im Jahre 1961 hinterließ eine Leerfläche, die erst das neue Tempodrom zu füllen begann. Auch hier mischen sich Alt und Neu auf eine irritierende, provozierende Weise. Warum die widersprüchlichen Solitäre dieser Stadt am Ende doch ein zusammenhängendes Bild ergeben, ein Ganzes, das mehr ist als die Summe seiner Teile, ist eine durchaus offene Frage.

BIOGRAPHIEN

Erik-Jan Ouwerkerk, geboren 1959 in Leiderdorp (Niederlande), studierte zunächst Biologie und wandte sich danach der Fotografie zu. Seit 1988 lebt er als freier Fotograf in Berlin. Im Nicolai Verlag sind mehrere Publikationen mit Fotografien von ihm veröffentlicht worden, darunter die Bände »David Wagner in Berlin« und »Neue Gartenkunst in Berlin«.

Andreas Krause, geboren 1963, studierte Germanistik, Philosophie und Geschichte und arbeitet heute als freier Autor und Journalist in Berlin. Im Jahr 1999 erschien sein Buch »Scapa Flow. Die Selbstversenkung der wilhelminischen Flotte«, 2001 im Nicolai Verlag »Im Borchardt. Menschen, Geschichten, Rezepte«; außerdem publizierte er zahlreiche Zeitungsartikel und verfasste Rundfunkbeiträge zu historischen und politischen Themen.

Antonia Meiners, geboren 1943, studierte Germanistik und arbeitet als freie Lektorin und Autorin in Berlin. Im Nicolai Verlag veröffentlichte sie »Berlin. Photographien 1880–1930« und »Berlin 1945. Eine Chronik in Bildern«.

Erik-Jan Ouwerkerk, *born in 1959 in Leiderdorp (Netherlands), studied biology before taking up photography. Since 1988 he has worked as a free-lance photographer in Berlin. Nicolai has published several books with photos by Ouwerkerk, including "David Wagner in Berlin" and "Neue Gartenkunst in Berlin".*

Andreas Krause, *born in 1963, studied German, philosophy and history. He now works as a free-lance author and journalist in Berlin. In 1999 his book "Scapa Flow. Die Selbstversenkung der wilhelminischen Flotte" appeared, and "Im Borchardt. Menschen, Geschichten, Rezepte" was published by Nicolai in 2001. He is also the author of many newspaper and radio items on historical and political themes.*

Antonia Meiners, *born in 1943, studied German and works in Berlin as a free-lance editor and author. She has published "Berlin. Photographien 1880–1930" and "Berlin 1945. Eine Chronik in Bildern" with the Nicolai Verlag.*

Bildnachweis:
Die Fotografien auf den Seiten 2/3, 4/5, 52/53, 82/83, 94/95, 126/127 wurden von Michael Haddenhorst aufgenommen.

bpk – Bildarchiv Preußischer Kulturbesitz 28 l. (Kartenabteilung, Staatsbibliothek zu Berlin – Preußischer Kulturbesitz), 42 r. unten, 44 l., 46 r. (Kupferstichkabinett, Staatliche Museen zu Berlin – Preußischer Kulturbesitz)
Matthias Hoffmann, Berlin 110 r.
Landesarchiv Berlin 14 r., 18, 25 r., 30, 33, 34, 37 r., 38 r., 48 r., 54 l., 56 r., 70 l., 74 r., 85 l., 90, 96 l., 98 l., 106 l., 108 r., 112, 114 r., 116, 124
National Archives, Washington DC 20 r., 26 r., 69 r.

© 2006 Nicolaische Verlagsbuchhandlung GmbH, Berlin
Übersetzung: Michael Robinson
Gestaltung und Satz: hawemannundmosch, Berlin
Covergestaltung: hawemannundmosch, Berlin
Repro: Mega-Satz-Service, Berlin
Druck und Bindung: Rasch, Bramsche
Printed in Germany
ISBN 13: 978-3-89479-262-6
ISBN 10:   3-89479-262-0

Unter www.nicolai-verlag.de können sie unseren Newsletter abonnieren, der Sie über das Programm und aktuelle Neuerscheinungen des Nicolai Verlags informiert.